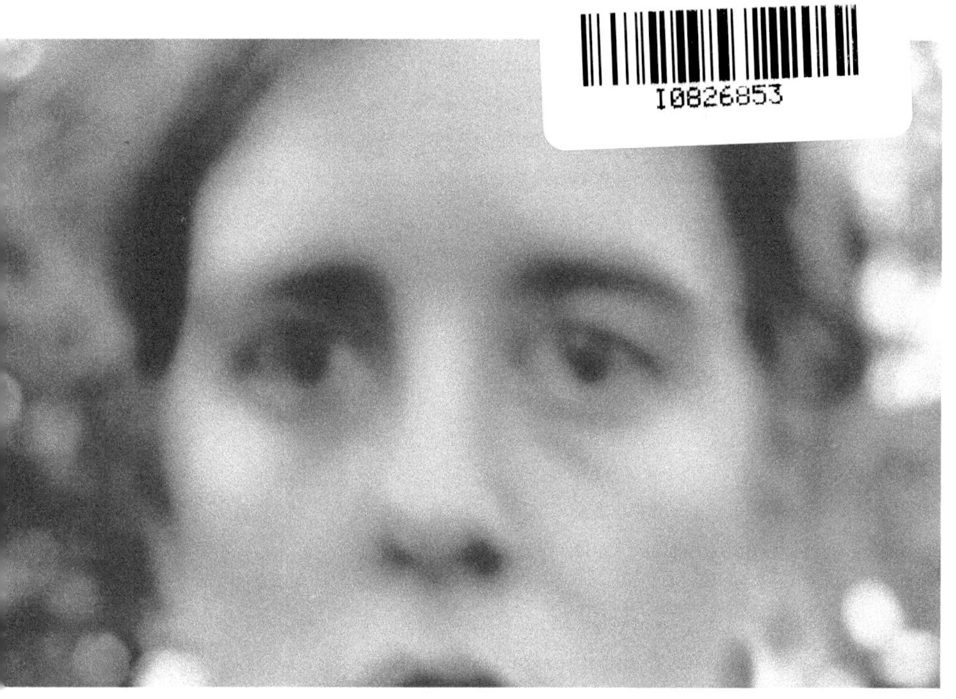

torment & soul

Cover Design + Artwork + Layout + Design
Bee Williamson of Bee's Boutique Books
www.beesboutiquebooks.biz

Printed and Bound in Australia by BookPOD

This book is available for purchase from:
www.bookstore.bookpod.com.au

National Library of Australia
Cataloguing-in-Publication entry

Author: Williamson, Bee.

Title: Torment & Soul/ Bee Williamson.

Edition: 1st ed.

ISBN: 978-0-646-96201-6

Contact Bee at: bee@hive.id.au
to purchase artworks
www.hive.id.au

Bee would like to thank and acknowledge Norman Lindsay
for the inspiration behind the cover drawing.

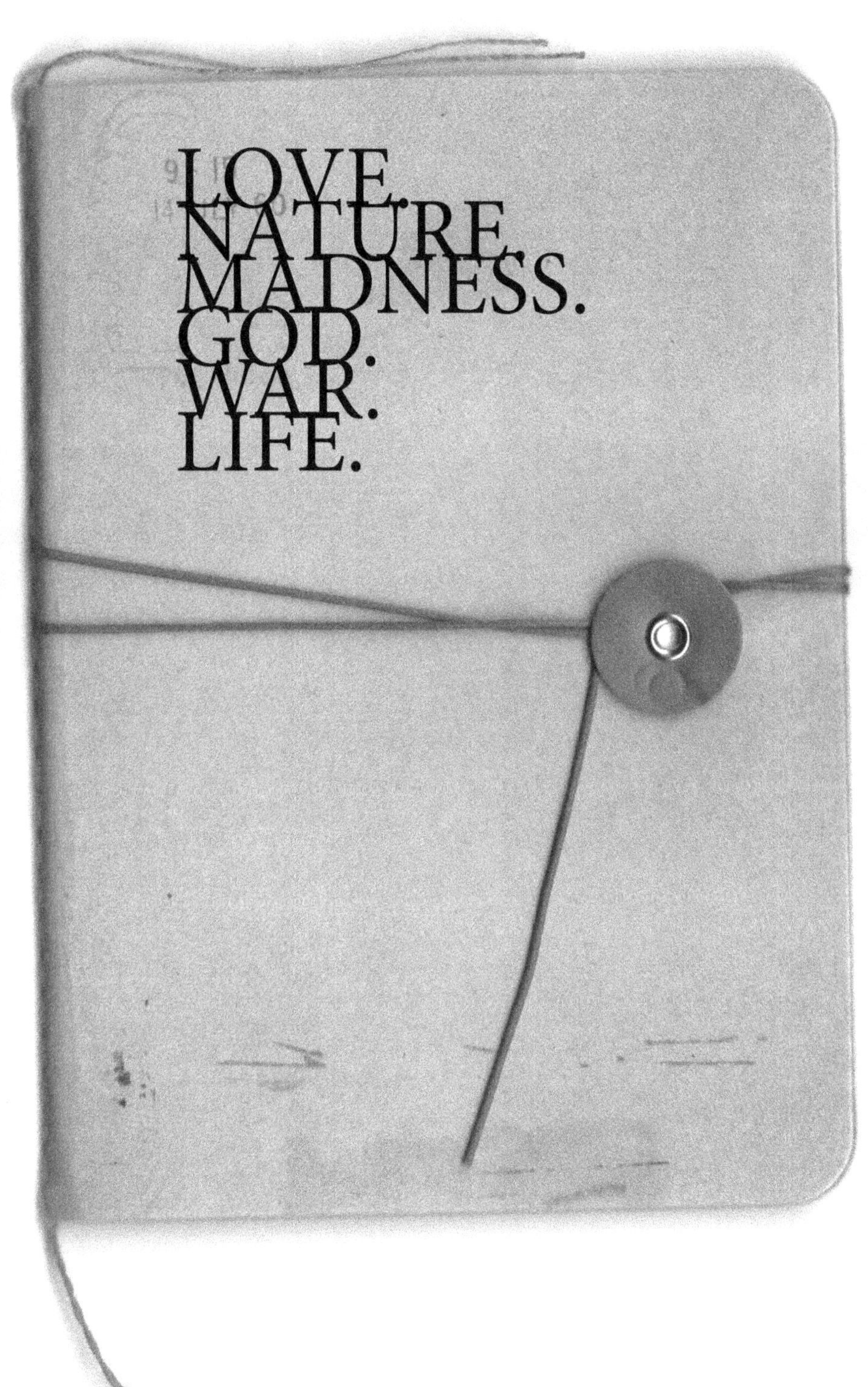
LOVE.
NATURE.
MADNESS.
GOD.
WAR.
LIFE.

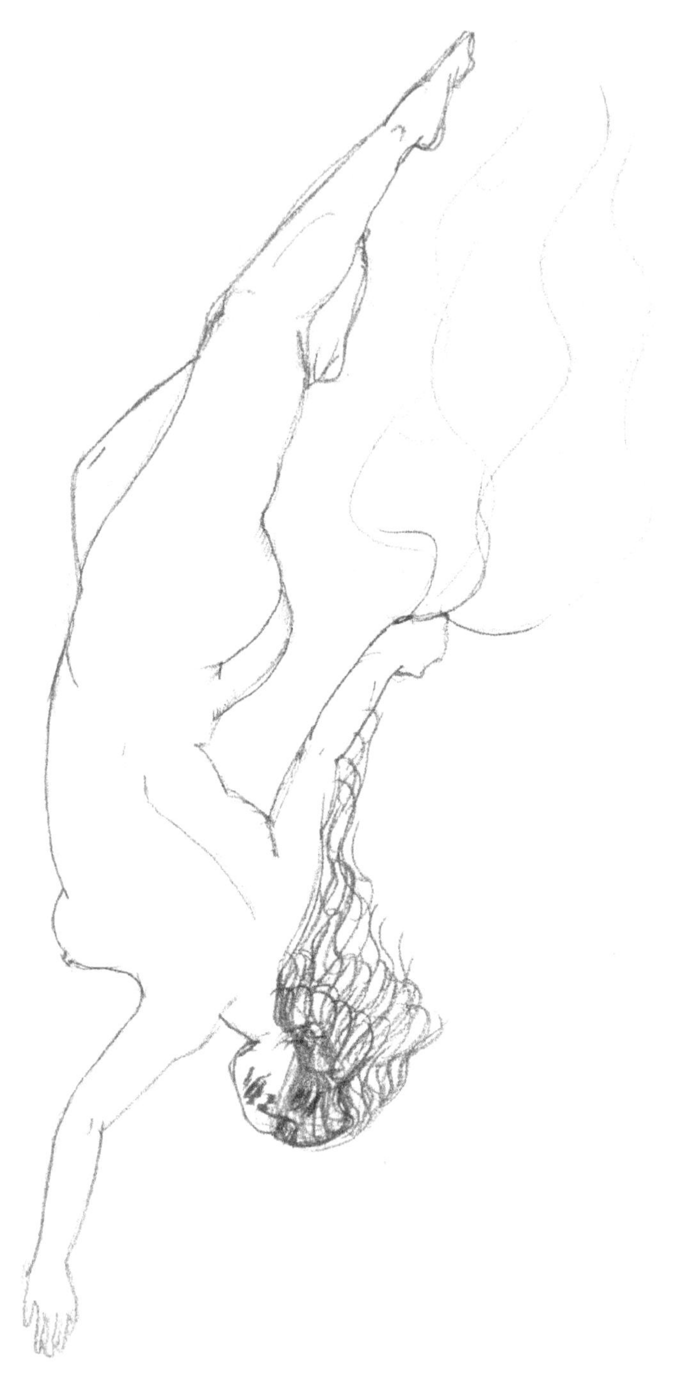

BIOGRAPHY

Hi,
I'm Bee. I spent some time growing up in Devon in the 70's in a converted furniture van and celebrated my first birthday at a Rolling Stones concert at Knebworth, apparently I was asleep the whole time.

With an early love of dance & music from watching my parents freeze to death doing a theatrical interpretation of the Egyptian Book of the Dead at a Edinburgh Festival, I came to love theatre down under at the Old Drill Hall in Mullumbimby. Yes, there is actually somewhere called Mullumbimby.

Back to drizzly hometown Melbourne, finishing highschool directing 'A Midsummer's Nights Dream', I went onto my own dream, a course at the Victorian College of the Arts. There I discovered photography, creative writing including poetry and 11pm hot chocolates in empty artrooms. A long relationship with the written word developed as theatre-love was buried in too much Lacan theory.

In 2010-2011 I spent time crafting poems as a 'Café Poet' at Pheast48, in cahoots with Australian Poetry Ltd.

okay. that's me.

Published:
Books I've designed and written:
1. The Immense Sorrow of Stars
2. The Hidden Self
3. Nature - a gift
4. I Heard the Voice of the Ocean
5. The Heart is the Garden
8. Shadows of My Neighbourhood
9. I Know Om

2011 - "Nature - a gift" launched at Pheast48. a self published book of poems & artwork. Launched by Nilgun Guven and music by
Harry Williamson.
2009 - "The Hidden Self" launched at Dante's, Gertrude St. March 8th - self published book of poetry & artwork with Naomi Downie. Launced by Nilgun Guven, music by Harry Williamson.

Introduction

The title of this collection by Bee Williamson, "torment and soul", from her poem "sacramento", hints at dichotomies of mortality and eternity, flesh and spirit, sensuality and intellect. Her poetry celebrates yet shatters this binary pattern, pulling apart divisions. No longer touting ourselves as masters of nature, we can rejoin it. The "transcendental consciousness" of which she wrote in her earlier work The Heart is in the Garden is an active force throughout her writing. Thus the vegetative world carries a voice, equal to that of humanity: "Roses kissing the light" ("Surrender"); "the fruit trees / giggle at her knees" ("Morning greenthumbs"), reminiscent of Whitman's Leaves of Grass, or Rilke's Sonnets to Orpheus and Dueno Elegies, in which mute divinity awaits Naming, charging us to hear and heed.

This sensibility dwells in contemporary fantasy novels by Ronlyn Domingue: "Even the loneliest of children find a way to tolerate breathing and... hear the stories of creatures and plants" (The Chronicle Of Secret Riven), linking Bee to an international artistic movement variously described as eco-spiritual, ethereal, gothic or neo-Romantic, with roots in classical mythology, medieval romance, Elizabethan supernaturalism (including that of Shakespeare's plays), the Pre-Raphaelites and transcendentalism, while drawing upon other influences such as expressionism. Williamson's eclectic mind may delight in a whirl of dancers with diaphanous gowns in Arcadian gardens, then plunge into a Film Noir alley amid stark black & white lighting and urban alienation. As such, she embodies the restlessness of both worlds.

Metaphors bloom in Williamson's laurel, and tend to be most resplendent when hinting at divinity. God (in his or her various guises) is depicted as "a snow leopard / glowing in the moonlight / on the cliffs of shale / soft yet strong / enduring / always / in us" (The Red in a Robin's Breast).

"We speak of earth time under a splendid banner", wrote Williamson earlier (in The Heart is in the Garden): a lucid moment rises, glorious and dignified above the vapidity of our era. Spiritual alchemy abounds in her poetry with references to Sufism (she quotes Rumi) as well as Hinduism, Taoism and Buddhism. She also calls upon Druidic, African, Jewish, Amerindian and Christian figures, interwoven with Aboriginal lore.

Bee Williamson sleeps in an attic. Her bed abuts a large, slanting window through which she gazes at a "night sky, dripping with stars" (The Monk), imbibing inspiration at the borders of dreaming. Her experience of random, celestial mediumship departs from the fashion of industrial writing, whereby authors sit dutifully at desks, staring at blank screens.

Aptly she writes, “Clever culture never looked so dull” (A man who loves her), stubbornly thumbing her nose at convention. After all, the Muse is not a creature of habit. She doesn’t abide by clocks, timetables and industry charts. She comes unbidden.

Williamson has been “clinically described” (“Sacramento”), by which she refers to her diagnosis of schizoidaffective disorder, both a gift and a curse, bringing great suffering as well as exquisite haunting; as Emily Dickinson declared, “Much Madness is divinest Sense”. Among Williamson’s contemporary mentors is Melbourne poet Sandy Jeffs, whose Poems from the Madhouse (Spinifex Press) she has found ennobling.

“Our bodies are made from / mud / yet our spirits / sing within the constellations!” (“poet & singer”) could allude to the Jewish golem, recurring with Williamson’s lines “silence / in his hands / working her neck like heavy clay” (“submission”), yet also calls to mind Oscar Wilde: “We are all in the gutter, but some of us are looking at the stars”.

Structurally, Williamson’s poetry varies. Some verses are extended metaphors that unfurl like vines, breaking free of form, while others are crisp and symmetrical, perching like embossed stamps, or colophons, to seal a moment into the soul. Similes abound, as in “from gully to gulf” (Jessie), often evoking imagery that inspires awe, in its true sense of respect and dread: “Lifted, like a skull / incandescent / left to rest on the abyss” (Adagio), tempting comparison with the uncompromising, sublime isolation of Emily Dickinson’s perception.

A constant thread of visionary expressionism moves through Williamson’s poetry. As Don Watson has observed, vision and visionary are abused so often in corporate manifestos that they joined the ranks of managerial jargon. Yet why abandon beautiful words simply because they’ve been misappropriated? Surely genuine vision can still manifest, even if only rarely? Consider the perennial words of William Blake, in a letter to his friend Thomas Butts: “Now I a fourfold vision see, And a fourfold vision is given to me: ‘Tis fourfold in my supreme delight And threefold in soft Beulah’s night And twofold always, may God us keep From single vision and Newton’s sleep!” It is in this sense that Bee Williamson’s poetic vision is magical. As is natural with magic, the discoverer might feel a contradictory impulse: to keep it all to oneself in obscurity, like a secret spell; or to share it, recommend it, and hope it flies to many other souls.

Louisa John-Krol
2016

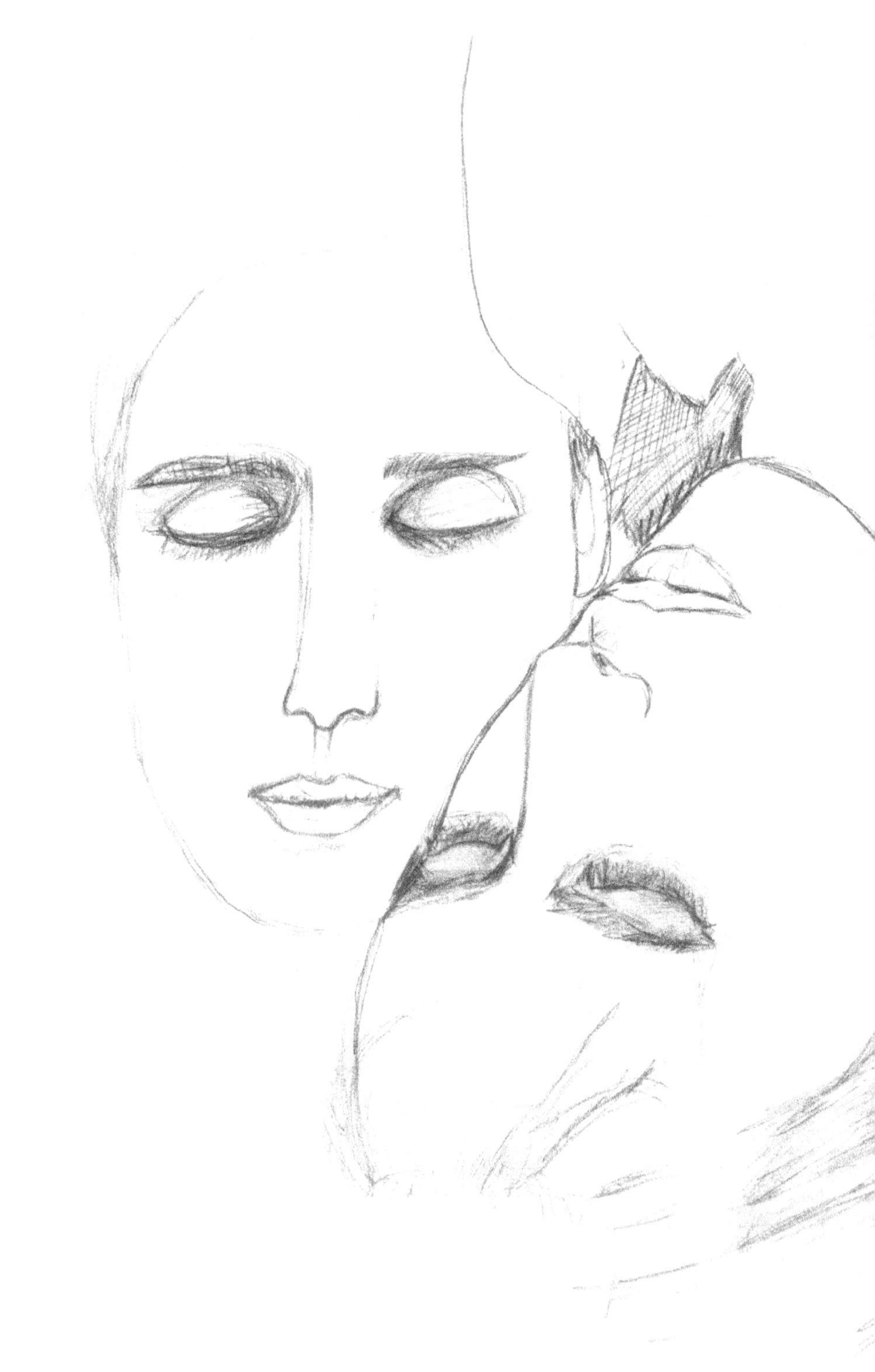

‘when you look for
God, God is in the
look of your eyes’
~ Rumi

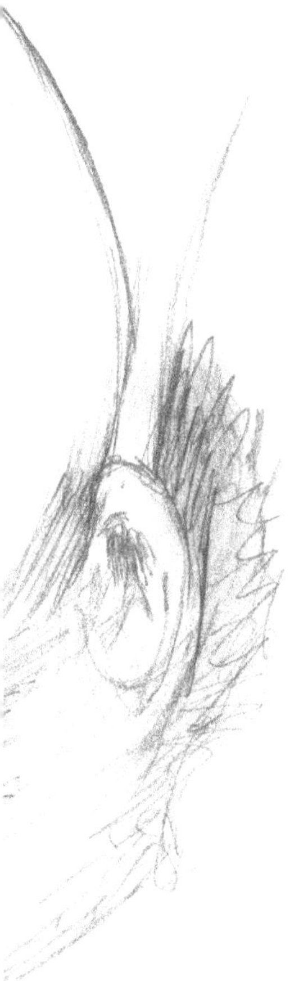

CONTENTS

Biography 5
Introduction 6

POEMS

LOVE **page 19**

1.	a dress dripping with stars	20
2.	A man who loves her	21
3.	Anarchic Spirit	22
4.	an ocean in his eyes	23
5.	And He Ran	24
6.	Bee Alexis	25
7.	Betwixt	26
8.	breasts like apples	27
9.	Charlotte Jane	28
10.	craving	30
11.	dance in my breath	31
12.	Django	32
13.	Darling, my Darling	33
14.	Dreams of my Beloved	34
15.	Falling out of my skin	38
16.	Father	38
17.	Ghosts - warm hands for Henry	39
18.	Harry- DaDa poem	40
19.	Harry's 60th	41
20.	Heavenly surrender	42
21.	I'm adrift	42
22.	Indigo Soul	43
23.	Inky Blue	44

24.	Law of Love	45
25.	Like a note	47
26.	Love III	48
27.	Lucy	49
28.	Maribel	50
29.	Marie Isabel	51
30.	Moonbake	52
31.	My Body is Ecstasy Trapt	53
32.	my man tormenting me	54
33.	Night Clouds	55
34.	poet & singer	56
35.	Romeo & Juliet	58
36.	Sacred Lover	59
37.	Sacramento	60
38.	Sleeping and kissing	64
39.	Sophia	66
40.	submission	67
41.	Surrender	68
42.	temptation	69
43.	Tenderncss - for Carol	70
44.	the bar opens	71
45.	this man smoulders	72
46.	Twilight Eyes	73
47.	When he touched you for the first time	75
48.	When Love Dies	76

NATURE		page 79
49.	And so my people	80
50.	And the bird said	82
51.	As She Turns	83
52.	As The Earth	85
53.	Farmer's Heart	86
54.	Friends of mine	87
55.	I See God In Your Toes	88
56.	I'm in love with a bird	89
57.	in earth's gentle hands	90
58.	like a lion of the sky	92
59.	Maori - Te Whenua	94
60.	Morning greenthumbs	95
61.	Mother Earth Part I	96
62.	Mother Earth Part II	99
63.	Mother Earth Part III	100
64.	Mother Earth Part IV	102
65.	Our Feathery Friends	104
66.	Poetree	106
67.	Raining	107
68.	Sickness & Fever	108
69.	Spider Woman	110
70.	the fires	111
71.	the rose of the everyday	112
72.	The Same Land	114
73.	The Voiceless	115
74.	Waratah	116
75.	When everything speaks	117
76.	Wisdom Tree	118
77.	Zula's Wisdom	119

MADNESS page 121

78. And so she washed me - the Alfred 122
79. as small as ink drying on Darwin's page 123
80. Beautiful Soul, Tortured Mind 125
81. before they knew 126
82. Broken Hearted Misfit 128
83. consolations 129
84. cracks in my heart 130
85. Defenceless Monkey 132
86. Episodes 134
87. etched on the underside 135
88. innumerable fears 136
89. Lunacy 137
90. My black dog 138
91. She-Devil 139
92. Swallowing calm 140
93. to the darling soul who never knew 143
94. torment & soul 144

GOD		**page 147**
95.	he being my God	148
96.	I feel the old God	150
97.	Into the Light	152
98.	Jesus said to me	154
99.	Jesus II	154
100.	Jesus III	155
101.	Our Hearts	156
102.	the heart awakens	157
103.	The Red in a Robin's Breast	158
104.	Who Left You Bee?	160
WAR		**page 163**
105.	Arab Uprising and Spring	164
106.	battered hearts	166
107.	chess	168
108.	Grandad	170
109.	Grandmother & Grandfather	172
110.	Henry's Words	174
111.	how do we forgive?	176
112.	Loss of soul	178
113.	Soldier of Love	180
LIFE		**page 183**
114.	A city wilderness	184
115.	Adagio	186
116.	amber sunlight morning	189
117.	And Jesus Said	190
118.	Awoken from a dream	191
119.	Beauty's Witness - for Brenda	192
120.	Because	193
121.	Blonde	194
122.	Blue Being Philosophy	195
123.	Brotherhood	196
124.	Butcher Bird	197
125.	Butoh	198
126.	Carol -Thank You	199
127.	Death & Convalescence	200
128.	Delving into her colour	201

129.	Diamond Girl (Jazmine poem)	202
130.	Growing Up a Pessimist	203
131.	Happiness	204
132.	He Dances	205
133.	Heart Sick	206
134.	Horses Feel Too	209
135.	in the dream	210
136.	Japan in Atomic Meltdown	211
137.	Jess - a billion walking days	212
138.	Jessie	214
139.	Jude's Garden	215
140.	just a bus ride	216
141.	Kelly B & Zula	217
142.	Leonardo's air	218
143.	Love is curing all my ills	219
144.	Black Dog ingenue	220
145.	Moon, star, wind, fire	221
146.	My fragments	222
147.	my own jewel	222
148.	Naomi	223
149.	Not a flirt in the house	224
150.	One Note	225
151.	Selfie	226
152.	slavery	227
153.	The Monk	228
154.	the op-shop-moth-ball-smell girl	229
155.	world in a tear	230

ARTWORK

		page
1.	Self Portrait - film photograph	1
2.	Dancer	4
3.	the lovers sleep	8
4.	T&S Woman Portraits 1 - Ophelia	17
5.	His desire	25
6.	Lady and her rabbit	26
7.	Satyr	35
8.	Languished lovers	36
9.	the kiss	63
10.	Siren	65
11.	naked man with fox	74
12.	Self Portrait at 18	77
13.	Tribal Bird	82
14.	Tribal Cow	86
15.	Owl	93
16.	T&S Fantail	97
17.	T&S Heron	103
18.	watercolour rose	113
19.	Tribal Dog	118
20.	twin souls	131
21.	Ottmar Liebert	142
22.	the muse	167
23.	woman portrait 1995	171
24.	Henry Portrait	175
25.	Secret Child	181
26.	Alien Flowers	185
27.	T&S Woman Portraits 6 - Juliet	195
28.	Angel dancing	204
29.	T&S Woman Portraits 2 - Jessica	213
30.	T&S Woman Portraits 4 - Imogen	223
31.	Sarah	225
32.	T&S Woman Portraits 5 - Viola	226

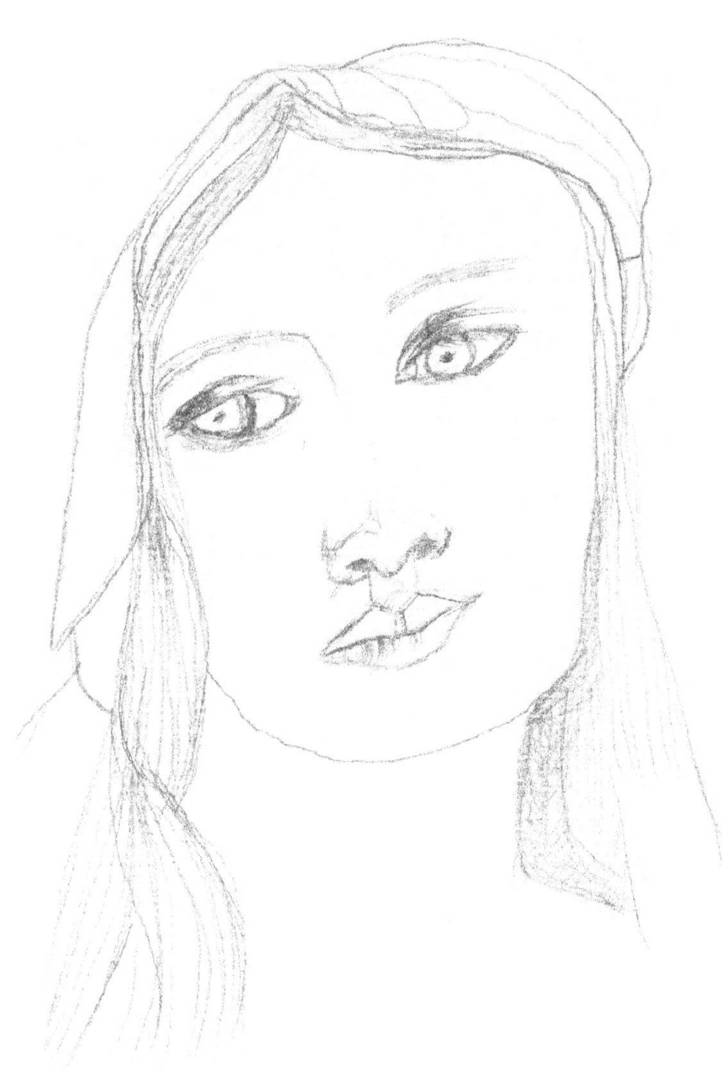

LOVE.
NATURE.
MADNESS.
GOD.
WAR.
LIFE.

LOVE.

a dress dripping with stars

deep blue black
shoulder length hair
and dress to the floor
dripping with stars
with drink in hand
and a lion's laugh
she mouths to him
a singular phrase
'I'm
home
in
your
smile.'

A man who loves her

Dancing on the walls in my mind
Clever culture never looked so dull
What's real
Is
The
heart
Look in her eyes
She's seen pain
And now her granddaughter
Is dancing and dying in love
With her heart's desire
A man who loves her.
Romance never looked so gorgeous

I'm kind hearted
doubt never looked so good
From where I stand
Upright and confident says grannie
But shame and guilt
Came early for me
Says she to herself
Alone in her soul's destiny
Single by the vision sense only

The death of character
Came so early
When a stranger Carol didn't know
Took us in
But became a nightmare
And drove me mad

Some twenty years later.

Driven mad by character assassination
At such a young age
Doubt drives me deeper NOW

Grandmother's eyes twinkle
With the stars of dreams
For love
To be cherished
Adored
Vows like to love and honour
Wished for dreams with sentiments
let me be your wife

Anarchic Spirit

And he smashed
everything
every filament
and point of view
with his anarchic
spirit
I cry tonight
as I say “goodbye”
to my spirit lover
who has incarnated
His voice reached around the world
his breath singles us out
each step – a sister’s gift

his breath
touches
my sigh
as my heart
weeps in grief

an ocean in his eyes

his hand in the
moon
an ocean in his
eyes
a prayer on
his forehead
a tender
reply
to melt
on his mouth

he floats in my bedroom
but I still ask him
to take his boots off
first
ha!

a moon
cradled in his palms
an ocean
in a teacup
twigs plucked
from his hair
wipe clean
his bed
nothing, if not
secure
dream
after
dream

is his hand in mine?
his heart eyes
stolen
my shepherd's eyes
my breast his hands
his heart my truth
there is a question made in the sky/air
I know this is good
when the air goes crystalline

My Sky His Sky
tentatively
my breast
on his breast
my sigh
his last goodbye

And He Ran.

And he asked
How do you hold
A woman?

And she said,
I can hold a mother weeping for her mum
Death at 18
I can shield a father at 16, with arms of love
I can hold a baby like a mother of two,
When tired and weary with milk.
Fatigue
I can't hold a bear that's throwing blue and white cups
At you…how can you hold someone that won't stop threatening
you

And she asked him
Can you hold me tonight?
And he ran
He ran his whole life
One long deep sigh of regret
Until he was no more

She never knew this regret
As he never knew how to tell himself
Slow down
hold her

and she said, in her sly black nightie,
what did the other man do? She is speaking to herself,
only finding that her temper has changed,
she is not his wife, or his bride, not even a friend.
He could not love himself
And she could
Not
Hide
Herself.

Bee Alexis

on seeing her sleep
I say
"You are so much
more
than you'll ever
know"

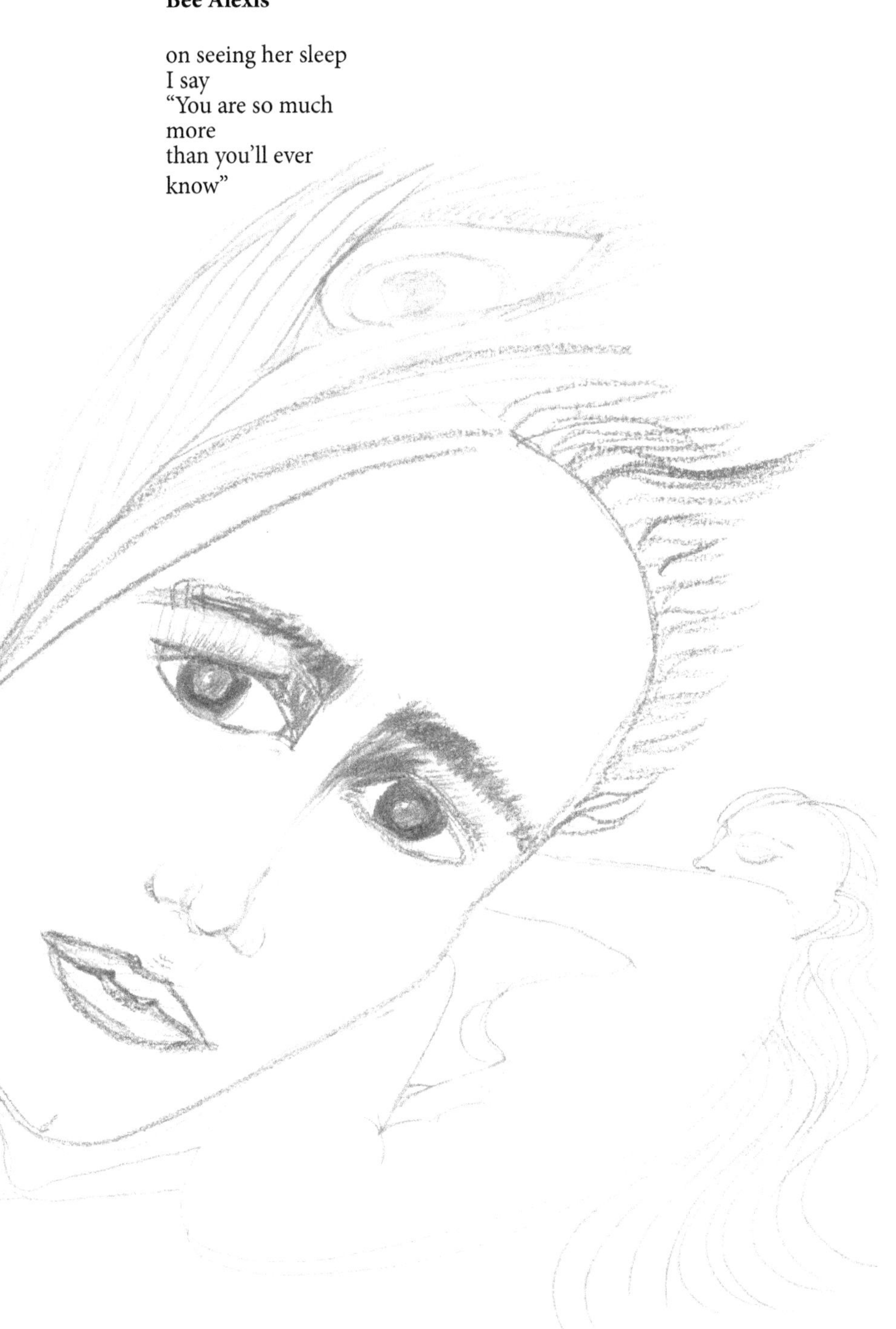

Betwixt

Bodies in love
betwixt moon & stars
I love him
like no other
before
or
since

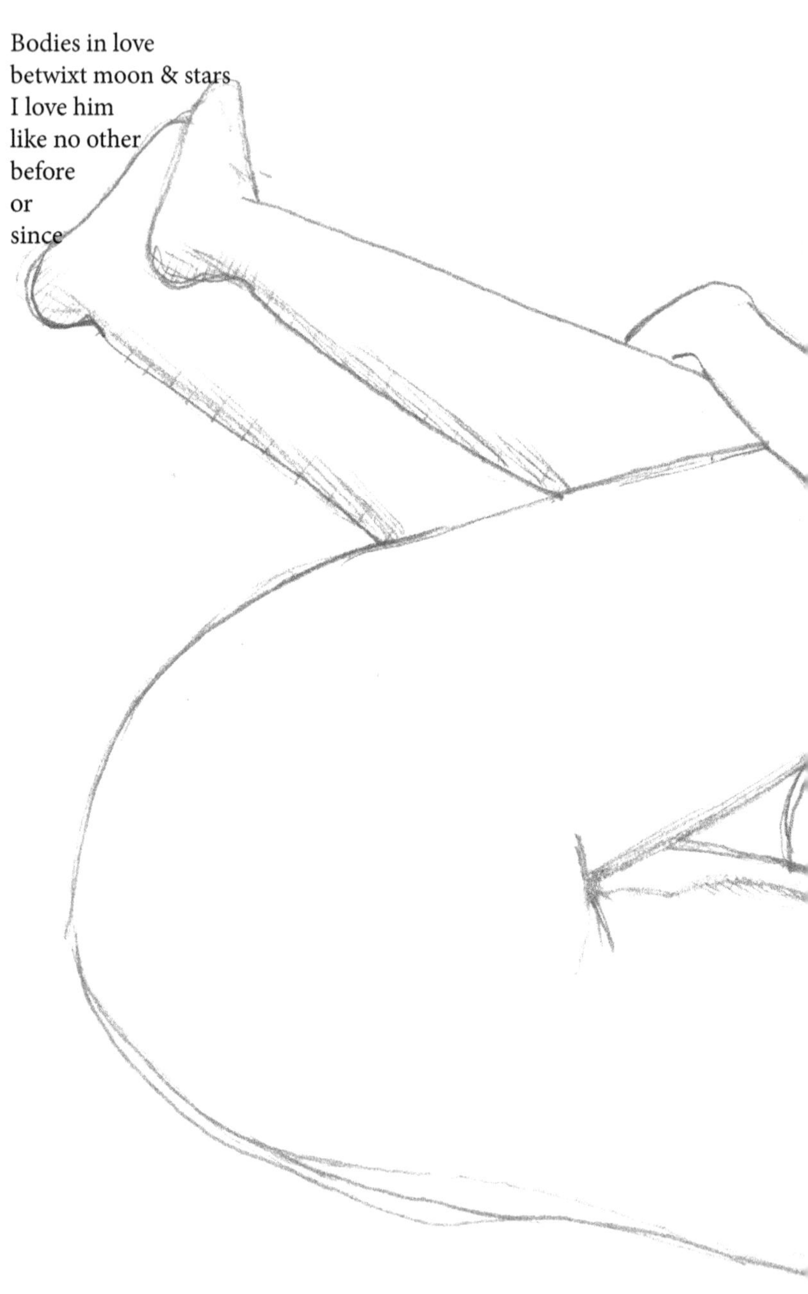

Breasts like Apples

my breasts
bare and ripe
as smooth as apples on a hot day
a crisp baking sun
on a summer's day

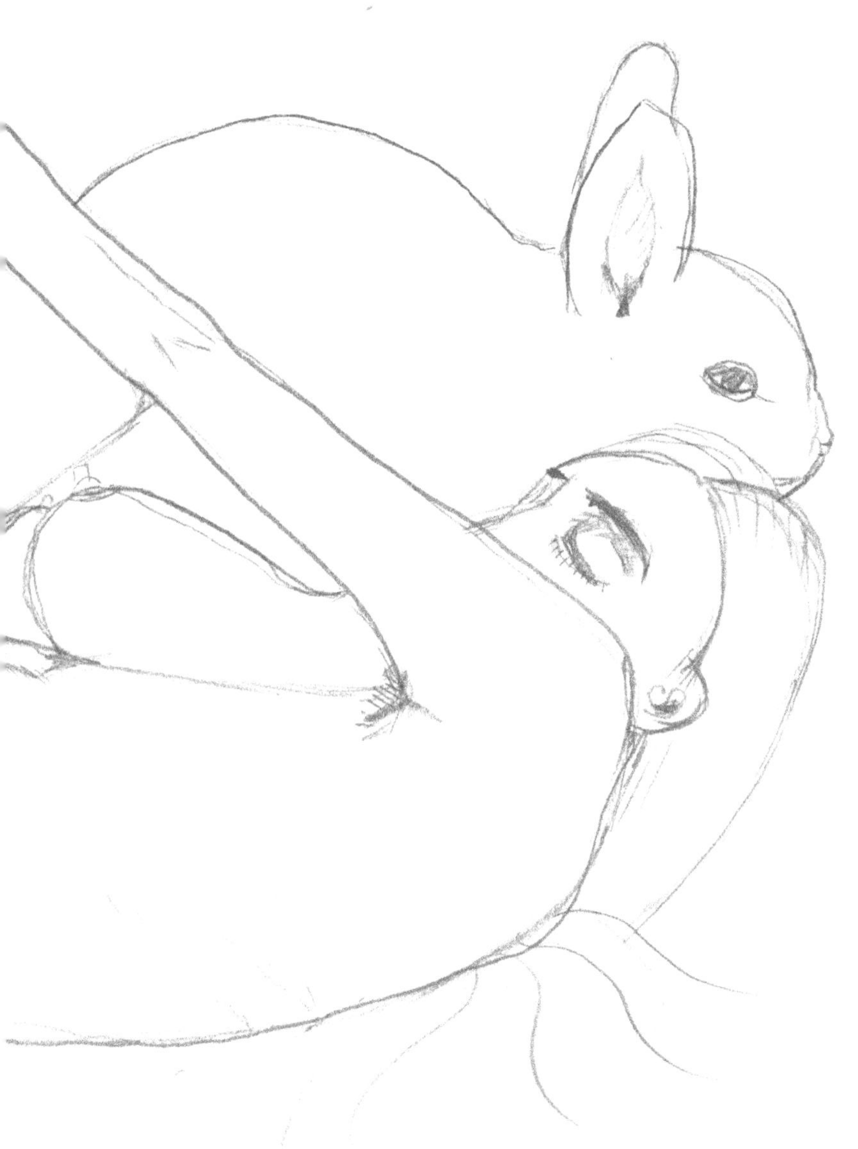

Charlotte Jane

She's got a heart of rich vermilion
And probable royal blood
In her veins as deep
As any ocean

Deeper than most people can swim

Taller than most men
Lovely because she loves them

And deep like New Zealand lakes

Parrapuramura
Is her mother's home

Alone yet not alone
Her lovers are many
In her head

Her heart is pure and sweet like liquid honey
She smoulders like black onyx
in a black man's ear

How gorgeous is she!

Infinite rests in her child's lap
With a cat curled up
content to have a nap

Tucked up safely home
yet
Mothering alone
Finding her life hard
At times resentful of the tardy waitress
The men who do not know
the plethora of weirdos on trams
down Chapel Street

How long it's been for someone to hold her
Without it being about their pain
Indeed she does proclaim
Bloody men she says
"they're all boys!"

She was always
my muse
and will ever be
with blue black
raven
hair

Her beauty shows
Like magnetic waves pound
Both bittersweet
sorrow and serenity
Finding her heart
in
a shadowy rose
She dances
like a shy
sultry
temptress

So dance lady dance
and shine
In all your true glory
letting the grey days
become
the silver
in your paintings

craving

touching her
was as
necessary
as breathing
air
today
if we felt the breath of wind
together as we lay
under wide white curtains
it was only between eyes curving
asleep in dappled moments
his time was finishing
the ships were calling
as war continued
and her time was beginning
alone
again

dance in my breath

where do I begin?

As stars fall
So did his
When his formless kindness
envelops me
His spirit hands
Are involved in tasks
Of pleasure
under his smile
Is a warmth
Under his earthly eyes
A soul's sadness
Even before his tragic departure

But what of this honey man in his bee's den?

As the traffic roars
And the birds sigh
I am trembling
With the thought
Of what this morning
Began
As heat streams from my limbs
This spring fever
Envelops me with
Wine in our bellies
Kindness in our throats
Form and formlessness
Bind as
Soul entraps soul
Then lets go.

Can I let him go forever?
When questions falter on
His fame and my shame.
Could I describe the face
That glows with the heat, warmth & passion of soul?
Ahhhh, dance in my breath
Brother
Lover
Soul diviner.

Django

What did I see when I looked in my
eyes?
I saw a cheeky man with a moustache
I saw a sadness
That no one saw the real me.
And django plays on
His heart real in his hands.

Darling, my darling

while on Earth
He has my heart
And in his arms
I wish I could lay
But until that time
I will play in
Your galaxy of wildflowers
Sing on oh sunny day
Or winter shower
Eat and drink wine and dine
With others
I will never have another lover
Like him
He discovers every
Dreamy spot of pleasure

Dreams of my Beloved

in my dreams
I am lofty
in London.
Yet, in my heart
the devotional soul
yearns
for his eyes
my Beloved.

he's dead and gone
yet in my soul he
rests.

in his touch
is death's
burn
of
ecstasy

so beautiful
so sad
is his demise
his rock star eyes

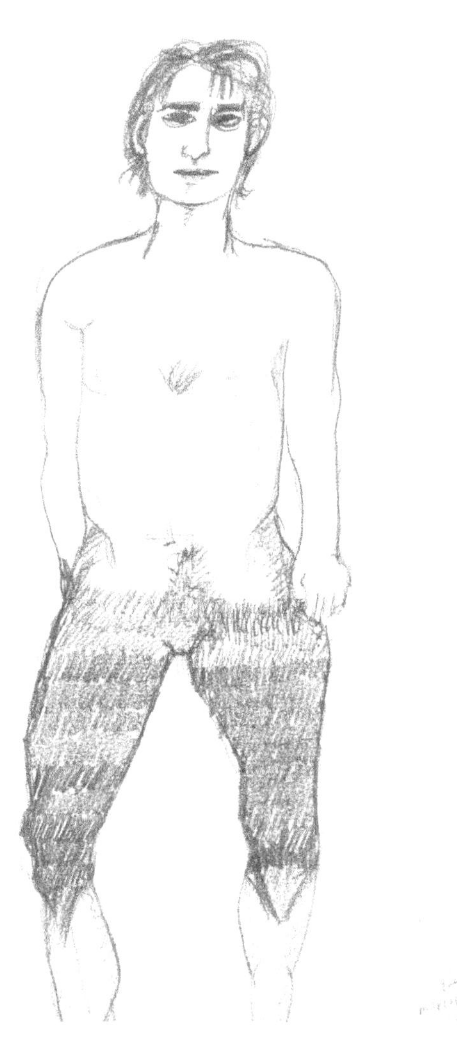

By the Temple of the Muses,
Where the climbers of the mount
Learned the soul's diviner uses
From the Heliconian fount.
By the banks of dark Illyssus,
Where the Parcæ walked of old,
In their crowns of white narcissus,
And their garments starred with gold.

Lady Jane Wilde

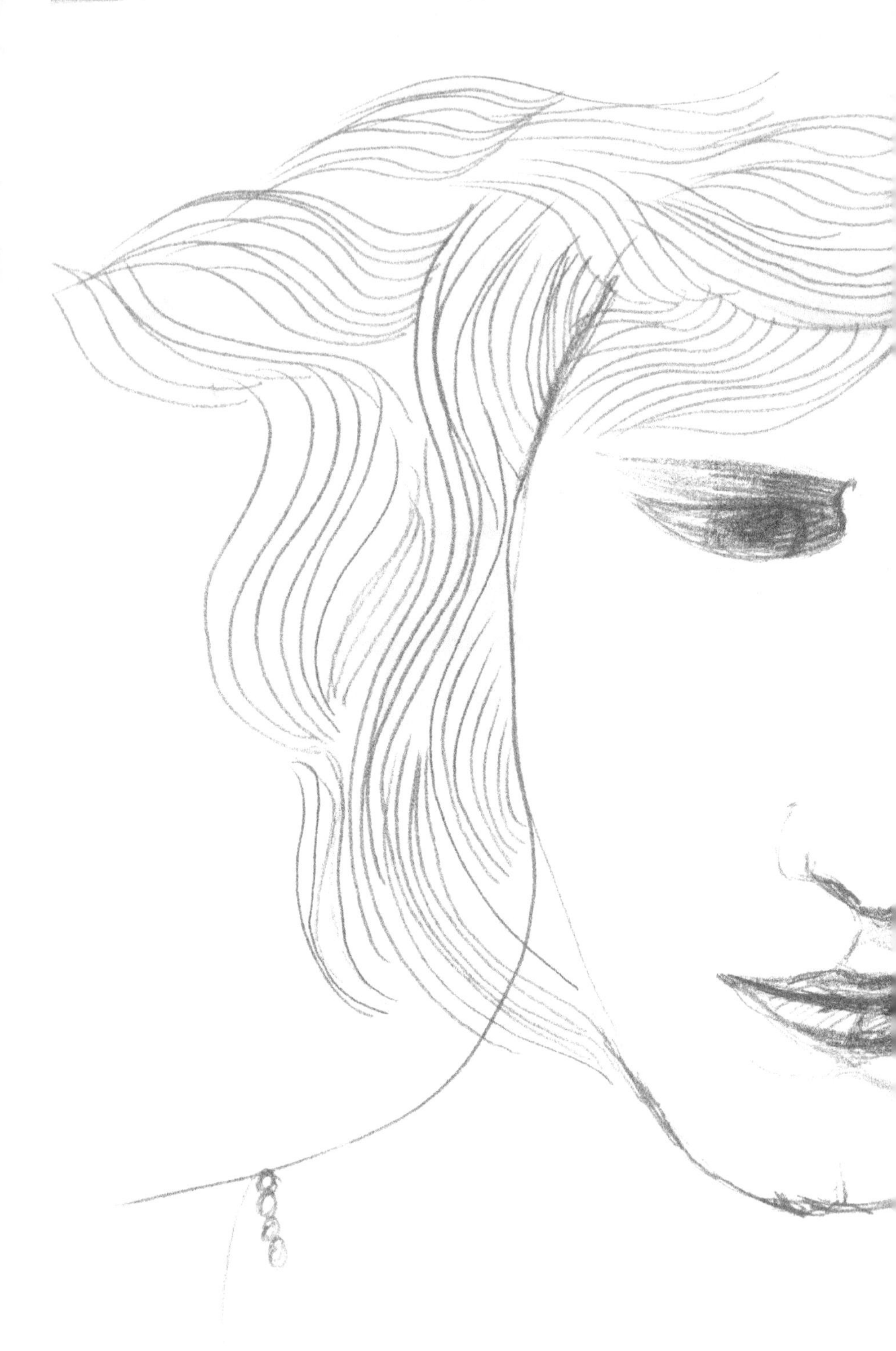

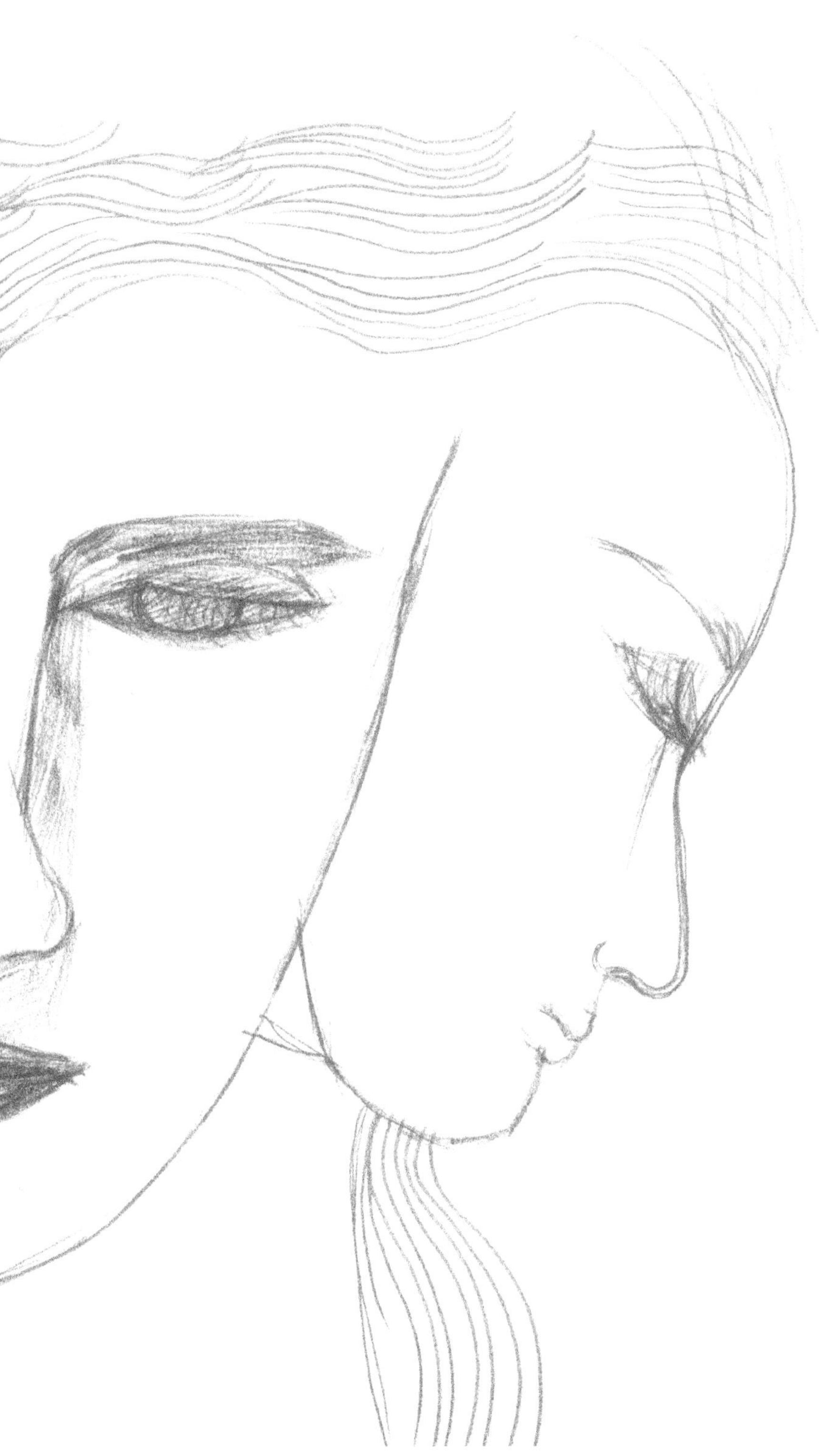

Falling out of my skin

his smile
and kindness
make me fall
so close
so close
nearly out of my skin
and into him/air

Father

In his arms
is all the strength of men
my father
has the eyes of a seer
and a smile
of a believer
make sure
he is safe in arms of gold

Ghosts - warm hands for Henry

the electricity is buzzing
in the walls
as I write this
the traffic of eight lanes
echoes like waves
on Byron's beaches

I sit under my lamp
feeling the electricity
of ancestors past
sitting beside me
the ghost of ancestors past
says, "may you find true happiness,
and hold it in your warm hands forever".

Harry - DaDa

He is like a ship
with a mast and a sail.

He's floating away
further from me
everyday

knit knit pearl pearl
she dreamt of you
and you came running
into her life with your big breath
and wayward smile

He is handsome
He is generous to a fault
and enthusiastic
gulping life down
breathing down
all the mystical colors
god has created!

He said to her "let's fly"
and she said
"lets fall in love with our eyes closed"

....
I love you
dada.

Harry's 60th

my dad
taught me how to love.
My dad
taught me to
love freely
show love easily
in the truth
of the moment
to hug in an instant
the heart leaps
to love freely
wholely & full
in the moment
and forever

Heavenly surrender

You made me surrender every
part of my being to you.
There are no words to describe
that experience
Except to say we made love
Like gods and goddesses

I'm adrift

in the
sea
of
his blue
eyes
and
sandy hair
as it touches
his cheek

Indigo Soul

he's not brittle
like the rough men of
war
his skin gleams with suppleness
he's not dead inside
like dead wood
heavy and burdensome with masculinity
He's easy to bend
lean into
fall into
caress
be spooned into
a supple man's limbs

my green man
of tides
wet
the moon in his arms
eyes like pools of dreams

Inky Blue

a wide smile
that's evolved
beyond the crassness
of what
men do
to women

a dark blue
inky stillness
still waters
with touches of
cobalt and aquamarine
and the edge
warmth
in his quisical
ways
finely tuned fingers
mesmerising to watch
as each note
falls on my heart
beat by beat

Law of Love *for Gilli Smyth*

In an intergalactic
Conversation (afforded me by my condition)
I say, "isn't it better that
LOVE
be the universal law?"
That the law of love should rule the universe?
That all things
surrender their grief,
pain, shame, illness
into the law of love?

I cannot communicate
Properly with these people
If there is no law of Love.

Love your friend,
But how do you love
Your alien?

My God, the Sun,
Is all consciousness
He is a feeling
That God is in a feeling,
That's when I felt one with God.
In a moment after kundalini in my early morning sleep,
(In September 2000)

I felt the Sun in the Garden and
I knew Heaven on Earth,
Was heaven on earth.
And it was the Sun,
Pouring down, all forth onto my lovely little garden.
Light travels
It travels, in our veins
As solidified light
Kundalini's light is
Sex

It is love
It is feeling

How does the human heart turn
On and off?
I have been deadened
By my modern life – of tv,
Computers, my boredom,
Knows only
sleep, work, rest, sleep, work
Protestant work ethic
Damn that sucks
Our hearts dry

Who stole our hearts
Who broke the promise
Of heaven and earth?
I, the white man
I stole the Earth's innocence
and
We ponder our navels
Why?
What I?
The white ones did to the Earth
We ponder and wonder only where does
Our heart lie, in each other's arms
only when I lie with him, in my dreams, do
I find my feeling

Like a note

He's like a note
One note
that stands between
heaven & earth
that stands
Full
Strong
Tender
Between
the first
and last

Love III

I declare
a love so rare
a peace
so fair
in my heart
I'll always dare
to follow by example
and be kind to those
less fortunate

Lucy

To the gorgeous soul
that will be born
in January

I love
and
welcome you
you little special one
am told you
can fly?
how high?

may angels guide
your spirit
to the playground of life
with Tali and Noey
together we welcome you
home

Maribel

She smiles with
eyes
that can not
see
allowing
accepting
understanding
her angelic
presence
lifting me
to home in my heart
her friendship is like a joy
is like nothing, like no other
any friend before

She is an angel here on Earth.

Marie Isabel

hold me
finding me
blessed to know
her
just to have
known her
I am nothing
without this friendship
I thought I knew
what true friendship was
but finding her
has been the blessing
of my life.

the thing about boredom and loneliness
is that it shows us
what we Love
what's not there is suddenly
or slowly
cherished

Moonbake

Dim inside
dim outside

breaking sideways
let's lie together
on the roof
of our squat
let's moonbake
our sweet sweaty limbs

coloured by cherry juice
London's warm sunset
twilight shades

I am your sunset

I am
My
mother's
reckless
gift

When, tomorrow,
you look for sun-days
You will find me
gone gone gone

Stoned and ripped
sideways
we lay together
on our London dank roof

I am your moonlight
touch between thighs
touch between fingers
linger on a smile
bent sideways
with desire.

My Body is Ecstasy Trapped

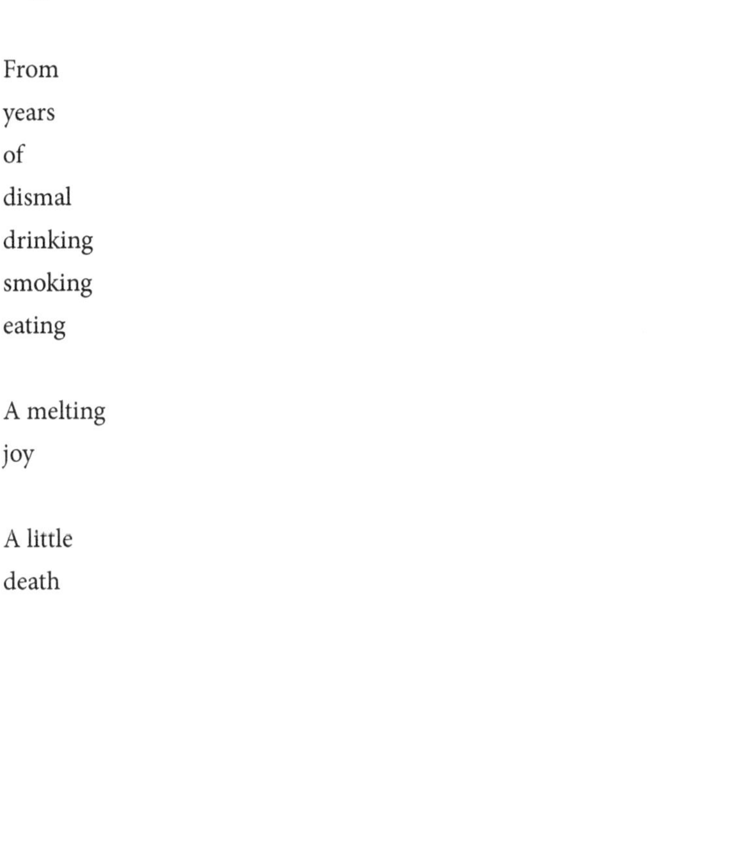

My body
almost transparent
with
heat
is
ecstasy
trapped

From
years
of
dismal
drinking
smoking
eating

A melting
joy

A little
death

My Man Tormenting Me

you can actually feel if you want to
says the man behind the counter at my cafe
it is my confusion
my soul sickness
defined by a man
who is no more a man
but a terror in my life

my heart weeps
blood red tears
one after the other

when someone says they will
kill you
just so you can be with them
what do you say?

my heart weeps
crimson
as the man I loved
is tormenting me in his
unwavering devotion

our love has crossed the boundaries
in form, in life, in death
it does not take the normal root
of love marriage kids house pets
it takes the journey of life after death
love found in the ether
I'm screaming in my head
so he will not kill me
to be with him while he is 10 weeks old.
it sounds ridiculous to me
but it is real
when you feel the cut of the auric knife
all that is left
is pale.

Night Clouds

When
You touch inside
My heart
Your dove's wings
Envelop me in
Night clouds
Forming breathless
Dreams
I am here
You are here
In God's hands
I float into bliss
A surrender
Into perfect peace
The warmth
That fills my arms
My hands
The calm that fills
My mind
As I lay,
Tormented from
My soul is split
His eyes are full of love
And his arms
Are an embrace
So warm
I will surely drown
You reach into my heart
And pull out my soul
It is a tired, weary
Burdensome mind

I am tempted by sex,
By food.
I am fooled by desire
Thinking it full
But
Finding it empty.
He did say
Don't make pleasure
your master.

poet & singer

Your soul
speaks to me
tonight
the softness
of each other's spirit
enfolds us

poet & singer
breath & air & pen
my Zhivago
a special friend
in the chaos
of empty contentment

we unfold
longings in the
psychic form
manifest
in tomorrow's dance
coffee
let's do coffee
and let tomorrow
entrance us
while I dance
with shaven legs
and think of your
thunderbolt stare

this psychic tree's whisper
faith & trust
in you
is the biggest leap of faith
I have left
after too many years
too many counted
hours of watching

your shoulders roll
on Youtube
your brown
lung guns!

kiss kiss
heart heart
Let's start!
the geography of my heart
has changed since meeting him
I feel new landscapes inside
my emotional coastline

our bodies
are from mud
but our souls
are made of stars

our bodies are made from
mud
yet our spirits
sing within the constellations!

Romeo & Juliet

a tale of two
hearts
that beat as one
star-crossed
and ill fated
lovers

Sacred Lover

he's diving through
the ether
to find her
she's waiting
with the light on
in her
heart

each day is an intricate
search for balance
between attention
of his spirit to detail
and her inspiration

the goal is to be as free as one can be
to dance and sing
and love

as muse
it is his beauty
as lover
it is his patience
as guide
it is attention to detail

all these things
I know not why
or how or when it will end

his sacred contract will expire
perhaps
how will I know the day
in my heart

when I worship
another
through
ART

Sacramento

when the dreams
pulse into light
testing times
when the jesus in me
is taken to crowded
chaos
inner city noise
is finding a love
yet sharing it
with only a bed
by the light
when solitary figure smiles
he's finding his blues in grey
as I find my soul in the night
and the day
I was bedridden with the decay
of solitude
born of self doubt

as we watched
the faces fold
into light
the soul in her eyes
the twin of his
"let me grow" she says
as she unfolds
her wings
of desire for flesh
and rest
in his eyes
is the dream
the soul
the twin of desire

It's a Joni day
I'm sitting by the window
in a smash and clash
of noisy life

that breathes
like me
but does not see
I'm clinically described
so my senses can
be abstract
and the houses collide
when the ages
ages ages
rushing rushing
to find a place
where both my spirit
is sounding brave
yet deludes
Joni days
torment & soul
weeping at my grandfather's
fox soul lying next to me
like the generations lost
places I found
when younger
younger still
these times are not where

I am
I'm not here, where it seems
crass clash, water pounding
I'm cleaning my soul
while the water
is cleaning the depth
of a Scorpio Moon
down this door
is open,
it has been opened
and lover stepped
finding my art
meaningless but
knowing I could do it
Now I paint these
dreams where
Titanina and Oberon
fight yet soul to soul
alike

dread parting yet
he is already departed
I'm dreading his words
that say, "I'm leaving"
dreading another time
where I float in the sea of life
alone
without his spirit
that guides me
holds me
touches me
tastes me
I float in endless oblivion
it is not a mother's hand
that holds
mine
in the sea of life
this invisible
endless ocean

"make your eyes soft"
I think as I stare
"make your eyes soft"
and bless your gifts
because finding a heart
(although invisible)
so divine like him
is finding bliss
in his heart
is Sacramento and pure

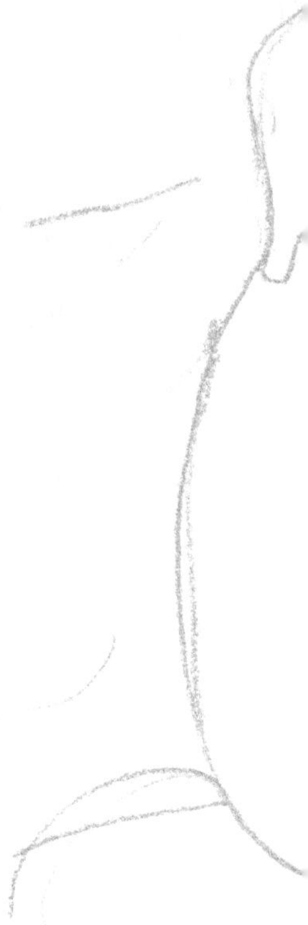

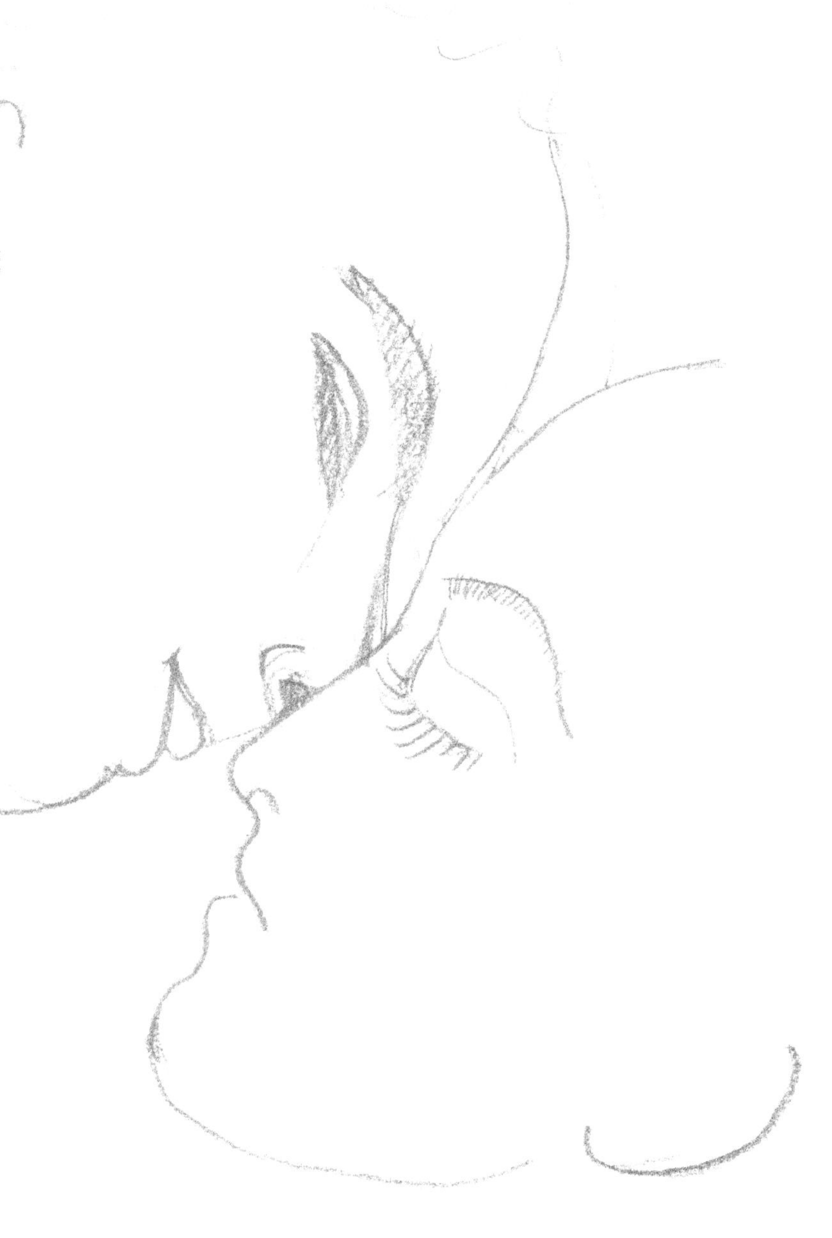

Sleeping and kissing

When you touched me with your spirit hands
Deep inside my core
Was a love that was finally allowed to be.

When he touched me with his energy hands
My body sang with whispers of 'more'

I have felt the love of a mother, a father, a child and friend.
and agreed with myself that I knew the love of a lover

but sleeping in his golden aura
where love became a small word
compared to the fullness of feeling
inside this body

sleeping and kissing
are enough

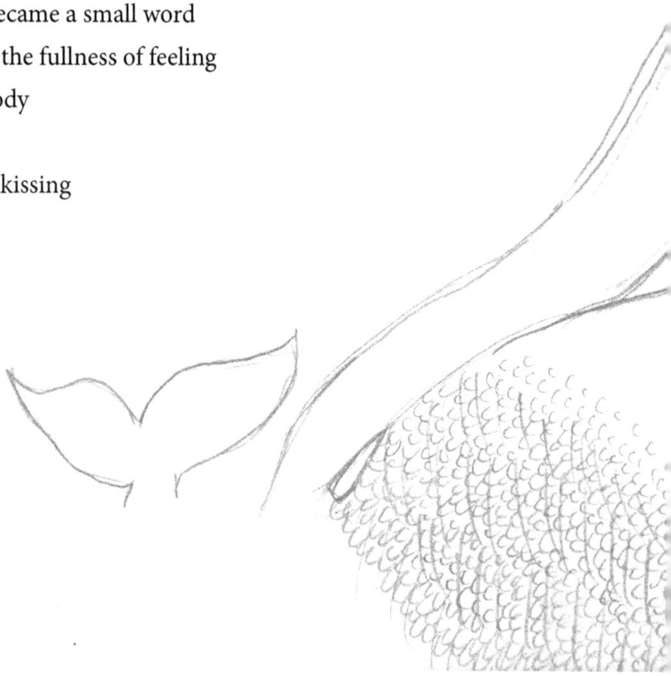

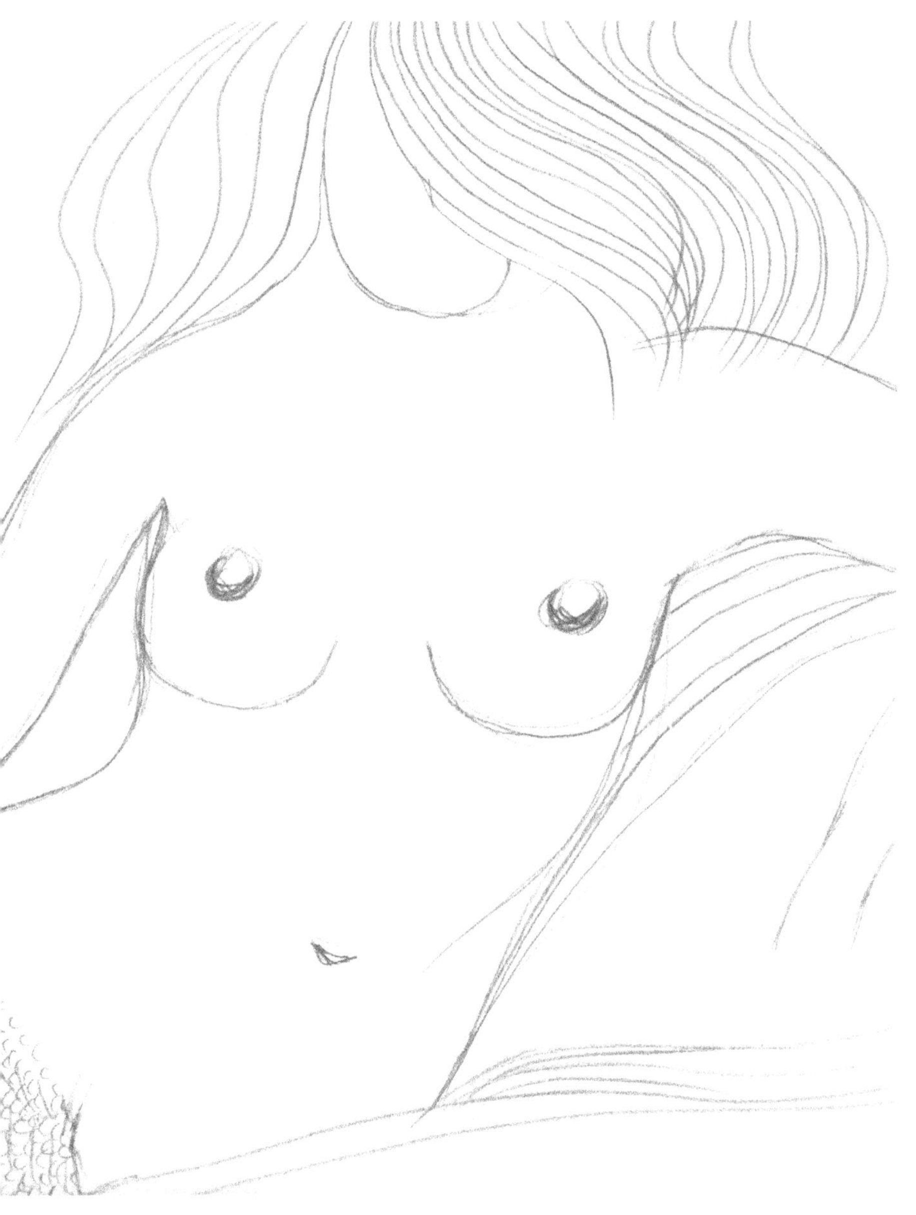

Sophia

eyes so deep
with soul
they drown
dark memories
of past lives lived now
in shivers
and breaths
So deep
with shining soul
harmony
in sound and smiles
like angels
in Love,
with
Love

submission

his substance
like an ochre hand in a ancient cave
strong yet yielding

her substance
like Spanish lace
black & inky
like webs woven, delicately in the moonlight

in her eyes
the dreams of
submission
surrender
and even
silence
in his hands
working her neck like heavy clay
is all their dreams of togetherness

Surrender

When I felt this warm love
It was as if my heart would dissolve
melt into the newness of wordless surrender

Or at times
pace so hard it would
explode with knowing
I could not breathe
without your music in my ears

My night-eyes are
diamonds
rubies
sapphires deep in ecstasy
deep in yours

what spoke to me
without language
your eyes
smouldering with a soul's
potency

love that finds
me
blinded
in the mid afternoon

alone
I think to myself
What brought me here
to this point?
Where I can love another
And not be betrayed
by my doubts and failings
my body and past

Empty
In plans
Plans make themselves
In kissed envelopes
Stained with wine
Roses kissing the light

Fall
Here
Into
Me

temptation

still, warm delight
like sunshine's kiss
each caress

in empty Italian cafes
dessert is cherry cake
with double cream

his downcast eyes
in his warm hands
her delicate fingers
elongated
rest on her chin

it's his temptation
to hold her close
his soft mouth
echoes hers
saying
'only you, only you'

Tenderness (for Carol)

And I am
nothing
nothing
without your love
I am nothing
without
your hand in my hand
Your smile
is my smile

stepping together
off the pavement
off the page
my heart
be your heart

My Mother
your kiss
is tender
in your love
for me

Your love is all that I can
find, to say
                    here
                              here
               here
is her heart

the bar opens

she's dressed in
flame
red
he's following the curve of her
shoulder
it's mellow and warm inside her
heart
and
again
swallowing his bitter shyness
he catches each shuddered breath
as her olive eye lids
lowered
melt
in hesitation

this man smoulders

his saintliness is stellar
his gravitational
force
swings women
over themselves
with
desire.

He lit a match
and struck a patch
and now he smoulders and glows
oh oh yeah!

Twilight Eyes

our twilight
eyes
dark
in the
mood
for
love

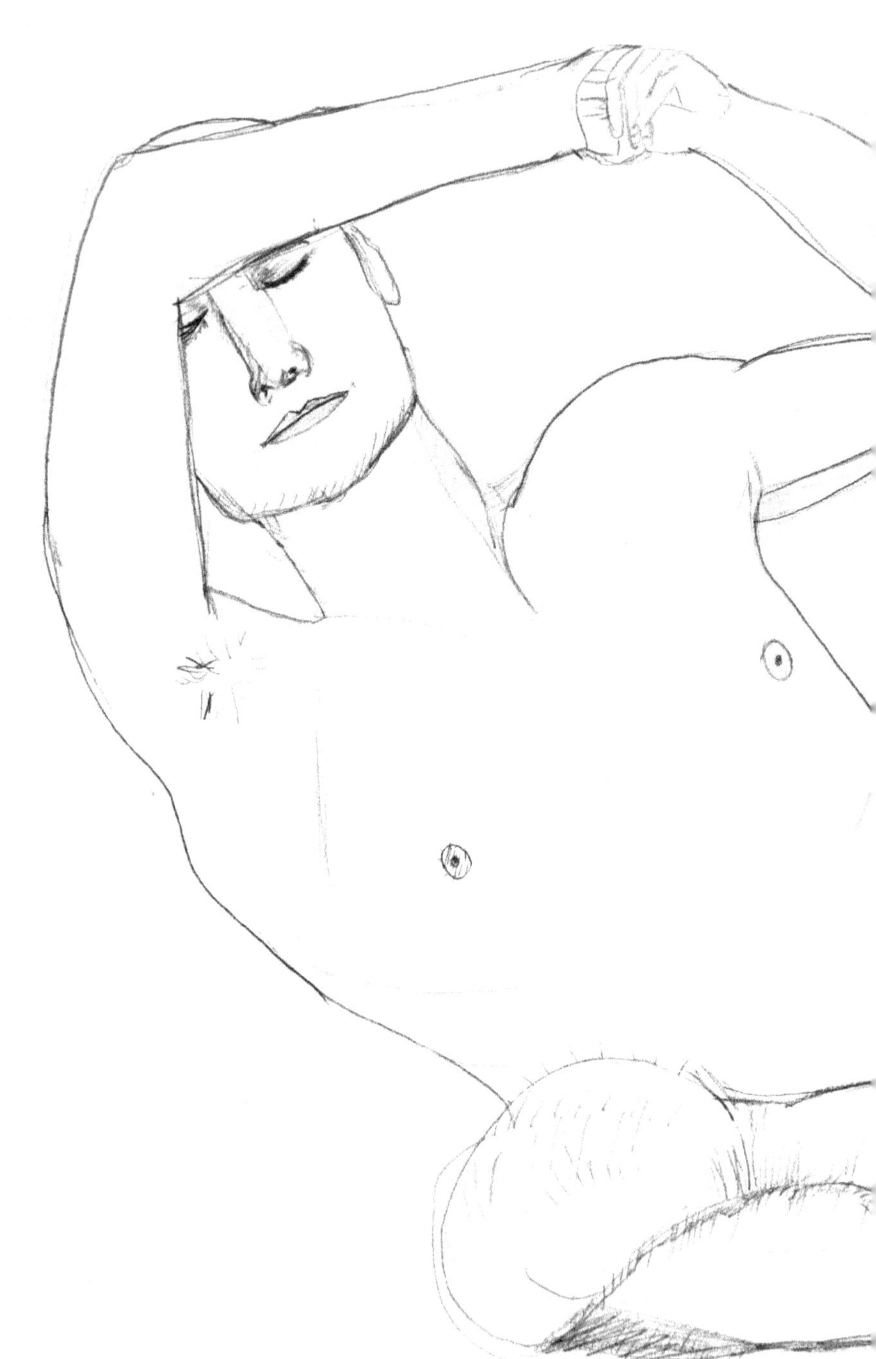

When he touched you for the first time

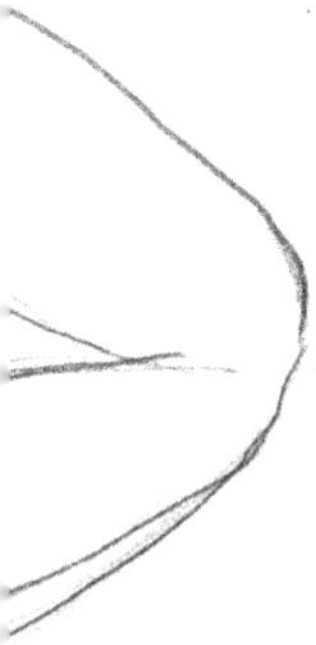

Did you swim?
Diving into sensations
Falling back
To lie in the waves
Blessed by the water
That blessed the birth of every child
That touches the ocean
When all things
Renew themselves
In her eyes
In his eyes

I exist because of love

"So do you, so do you."

My darling you felt the waves
the water
the ocean
when those tears broke on your cheek
and I couldn't kiss you any more

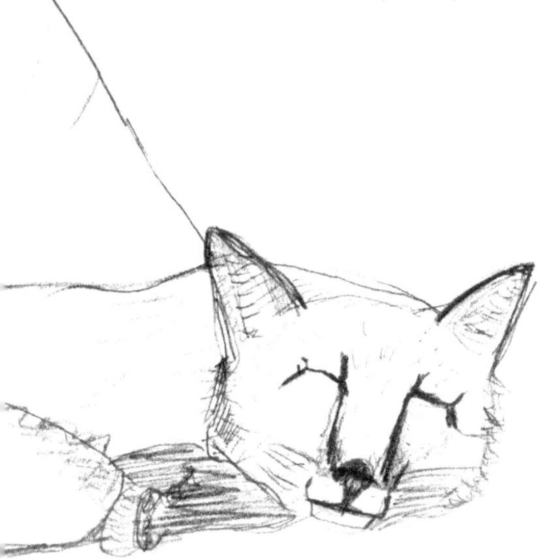

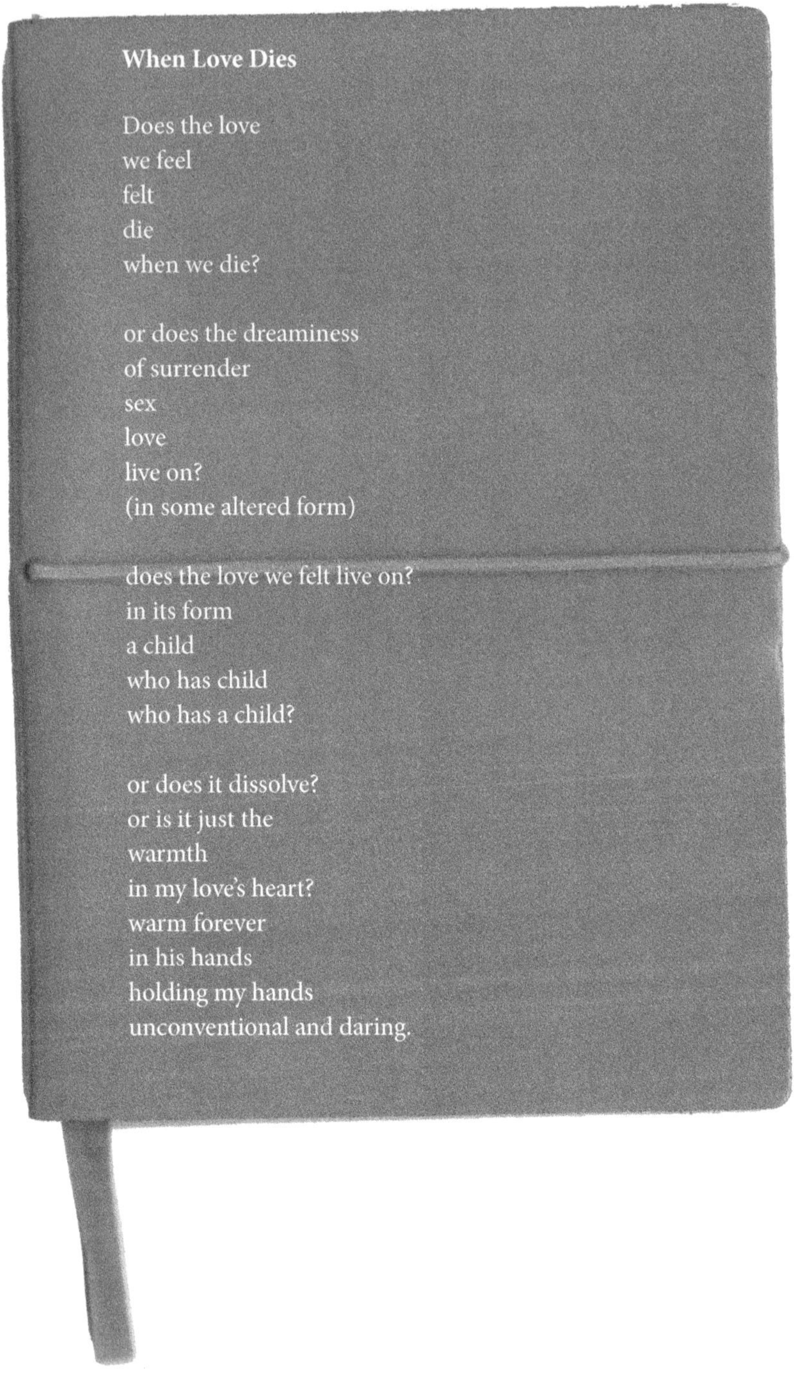

When Love Dies

Does the love
we feel
felt
die
when we die?

or does the dreaminess
of surrender
sex
love
live on?
(in some altered form)

does the love we felt live on?
in its form
a child
who has child
who has a child?

or does it dissolve?
or is it just the
warmth
in my love's heart?
warm forever
in his hands
holding my hands
unconventional and daring.

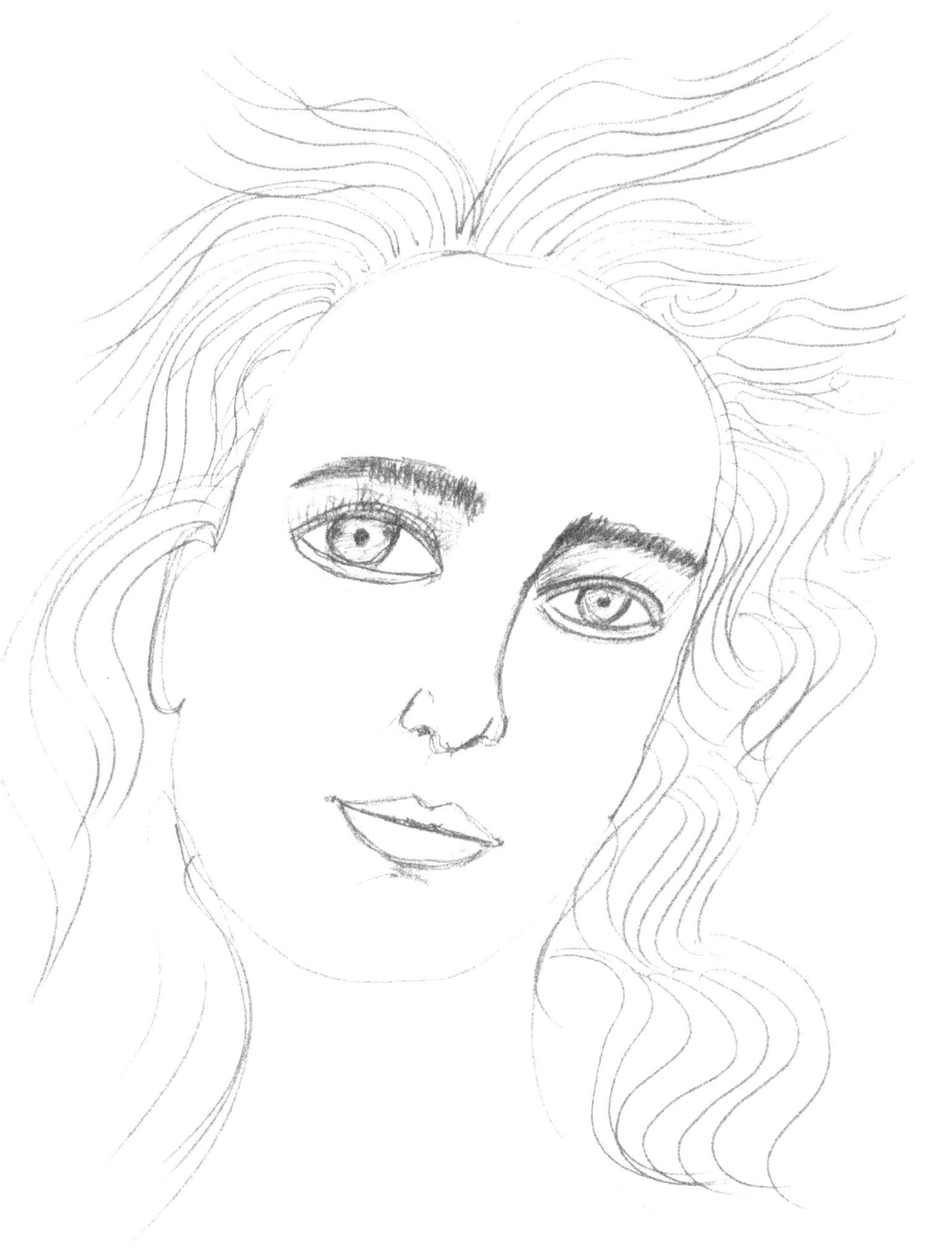

LOVE.
NATURE.
MADNESS.
GOD.
WAR.
LIFE.

NATURE.

And So My People - Tsunami

And so my people
My many people
Before me
Echoing every breath
Echoing every sigh
Have walked the
shore before me

But my people
did not see today
today they did not see
The ocean
Rise up ten storeys
And crash
With black magnitude
Upon every easterly foreshore town

At every moment
Her eyes flashed
Around to see the
Welling of cars, soil, sand,
Boats, houses and rubble
Death's debri

Contained in a wave
Soundless in its history
Never seen
Before or since

Struck by news
I sit bewildered
And in tears for moments
that stretch to days
of disaster
As the images pour forth

Tokyo
I have always had an affinity
And its ancient artistic proud culture
Dreams of the cherry-blossom festival
tugged my heart

But to see her island
Smashed senseless
Green houses look like pipe cleaners
Toy cars soaking in a huge bath
Alongside red toy planes

I am looking to the
Horizon as the sea
Washes towards me faster and faster
It is sensing its victory
Harnessing its strength
Against us
But is it a force to fear
Always?

I see the water
Rush up to me and I hear cries like
Gulls in the distance

I did not survive and
my village is destroyed

in her counterpart
I have visions
But as her innocence
Is pulled from her heart
Like a butoh white bandage
Only sand will be
Her grave

And the bird said
"what do you have doors for?"

you see
birds don't have doors
they have branches
open to the sky

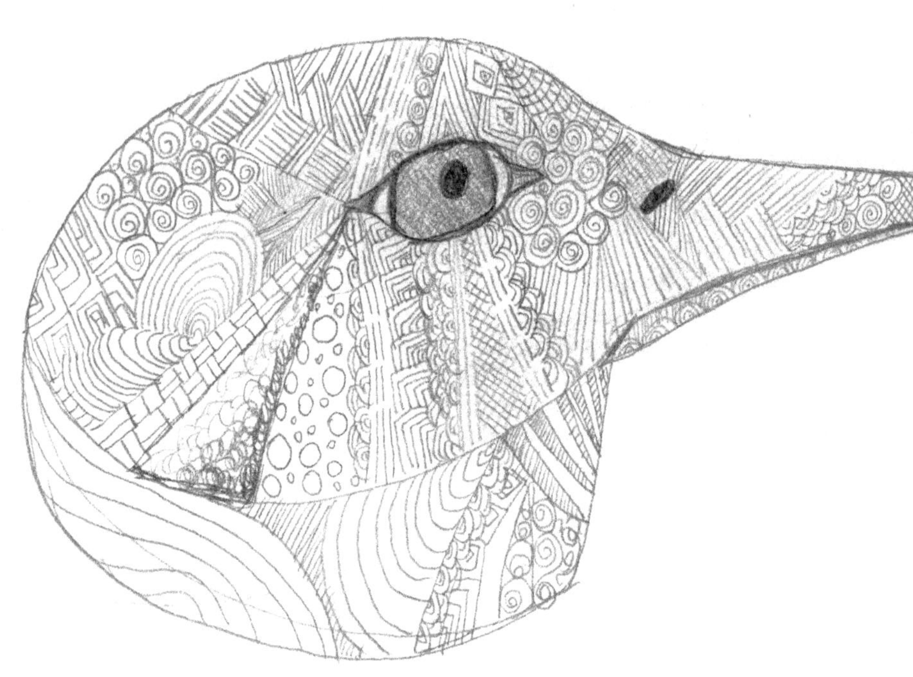

As She Turns

heaving her bossom
of bright blue air
her tides bulge
at the moon's insistence

I am hanging on
upside down
inside out
back to front
gripping onto my
blue sphere

oceans rising to warm the South
with tides pulling to clean the bays
of the North

Blue planet plundering
skip to our destiny
of coal seam water
on fire
while the rivers boil and our birds
die

outrage!
in keeping herself mellow with pills
my mind's awake now
and I'm seeing
fracking
and the fury fills every part of me

we do not know the balance
we do not know what we do
by all our short-term greed

nothing of ourselves
is enough
for our insatiable hunger
and so we plunder underground

not in my name
never in Her name

you tell us it is safe
in our beds
as you tuck us up
in poisoned sheets
flaming water for our dogs, cattle, sheep
in the paddocks
and grazing lands

As The Earth

when she will die
she knows
none, but few, will survive
breathe her last breath
and sigh her last sigh
and wave goodbye

Farmer's Heart

I have a farmer's
heart
for the deep dewy
eyes of a calf
I have a Red Indian's love
for soul deep eyes
of a fawn
I have a bushman's
heart
for the black swan
with its proud bearing
the walkabout
the sky burning with
direction
and instruction.

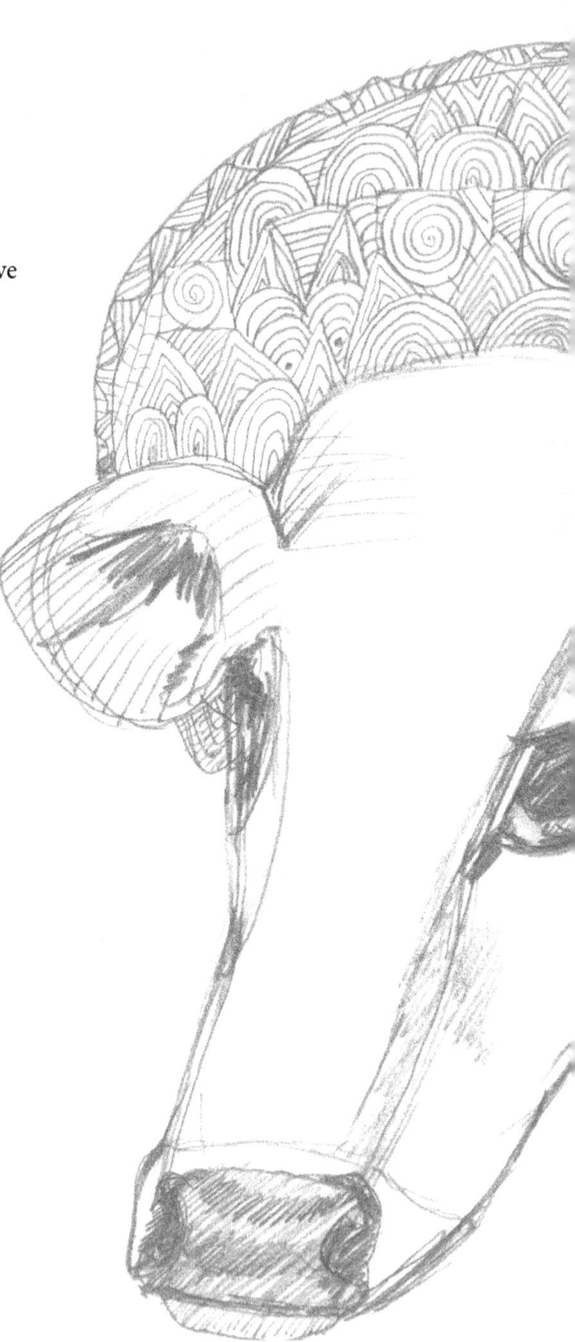

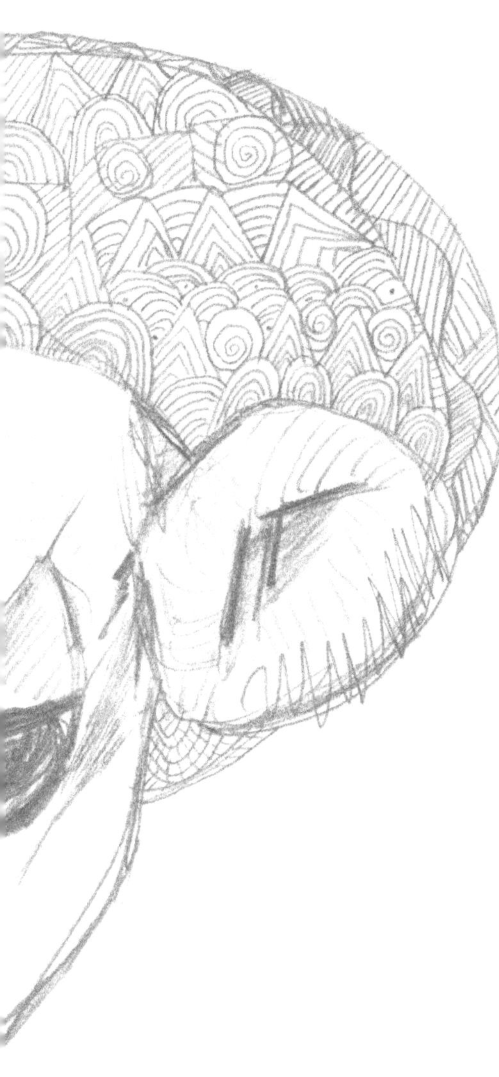

Friends of mine

are spooning up
in their bills
toxic crude oil

why did it come to this?
when nothing is
as important
as the plentiful supply
of plastic bags

Pacific is a waste dump
plastics dumped
for our daily waterbottles

a friend said
he didn't want to live
to see the day
we sold water
and bought air
but we did
but we did

I See God In Your Toes

when my grandad
said “I see God
in your toes”
painted to shimmer
like pearls of the ocean
I said
I see the beak of God
the wing of God
in his tail
the swish of God
and the glint in his orange eyes
the nose that smells
a thousand scents
I see God in the
red breast of a robin
the trunk of a Indonesian elephant

sleeping on an island
below me is the dust
of time
away in my mind
bed, a peaceful haven

I'm in love with a bird

delicate in his approach
to the food
he sits atop a feed bowl hanging in the tree
profound sorrow emanates
from his slow and deliberate
munching
from where I sit, he is shadowed
by the weeping myrtle
he looks like the soft face of a seal,
knowing
I ask him, 'what is your sadness from?'
'it is her, she doesn't see, this, this, is what we need.'
a soft warm gaze that cares, and tries to understand.
'we need you.'

In Earth's Gentle Hands

I'm like a slaughtered deer

I'm optimistic
I must be
I may have one day
mentally pain free
a week.
I might have
a moment a day
where I'm not threatened, hated, despised
by my army of voices.

I did not ask for this.
I did not go seeking out
horrendous threats to my sanity.

it was a wrong turn some where
a mistake not noticed
it was a stupid person's good advice
or stupid advice from a good person.

Can I break down the breakdown?
I would have seen a therapist
I would have sought help
I wouldn't have done six hours of meditation a day
unsupervised

I would have said the words,
"I've just had kundalini"
if I'd know the term
the experience at the time.

when you take a wrong turn,
do you ask for help?
I didn't.
And that was the biggest mistake
I went mute, frozen in primal fear,

catatonic, lifeless like a slaughtered deer.
near death
there was
no body
no jesus
no buddha
just me in my grey room
posturing rigid on the floor
48 hours to live
there was the sun
and the sun spoke with warmth
and no words.
it didn't need to.
if I could flood the halls of the HDU

If I could lie in a lake with lilies bordered with poppies
I would have awoken and said
"nature is my guide,
and my only friend,
when all deities have ceased to exist in my heart,
she calls me back,
with her possums and their soul eyes
she has in every creature that has ever lived,
here, with us.
If I could have heard from outside my padded cell,
I would have heard the bird songs calling me home.
Each eye of each bird a reflection
but never a copy of the other.
Her song, my soul's warmth.
Goodness in their guidance.
Love is simple in their hearts.
As is mine.

Beyond us, we would see the mountain
and valleys closer, and she would call me there,
and show me that I may swim in her reed bed
small, timid and shy,
and I could say to her,
"I just want to look at YOUR sky, mother".

like a lion of the sky

his majestic wings
of white and silvery grey
sweep across
the dark night sky
his talons bared
a mouse far off
seeing all that
cannot be shared
his eyes
a piercing stare
Owl of mine
father's father's totem
shares the love
of the other's
spirit eyes
and spirit tongue
mischievous and proud
like a lion of the sky

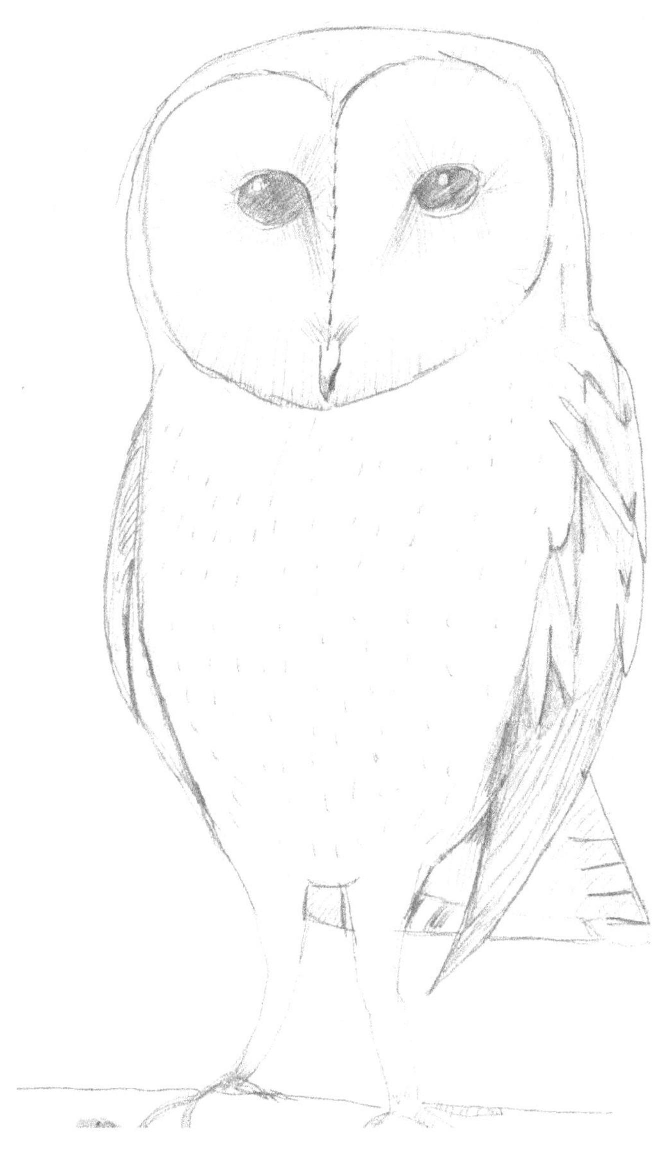

inspired by great-uncle R Duffield's drawing

Maori - Te Whenua

it is time for us to listen
to the Maori
chiefs, as they
raise their voices
and tell the world
their purpose
here, 'we have gifts'
kauri shell
whale bone
and fern stem

Earth, Te Whenua
is one
we are many
countries
we come from
Earth is Our place,
our territory
Let's demand we respect her
gently.

Morning greenthumbs

the fruit trees
giggle at her knees
as she prunes
the vines & caresses
the leaves
no snake will come near
as the trees have said
keep clear

Mother Earth Part I

Her glaciers
White
The jewelled oceans
Framed by golden sands
Her flora & fauna
Bright
Her flames of sunsets
At night
Her gifts of perfumed
Frangipani and magnolia
Each flower
Is her husband's delight
The sun
Soothing her weary
Shoulders of blue sky cool night
Breaking free her
Fight of cancerous mines
Fracking delusions
Oozing filth in her rivers
From the human desire
For MORE
Shinier and shinier
Things that go
BLING
Her beaches bare
With her trust & love
And all of us
Naked
Really
Without
Her
Love
She is kindness and warmth
But her fury
Makes us dance
In despair, as
We wince in pain, as each tsunami strkes again
These generations are a witness
To her grief
And sheltered
In our stupid beliefs

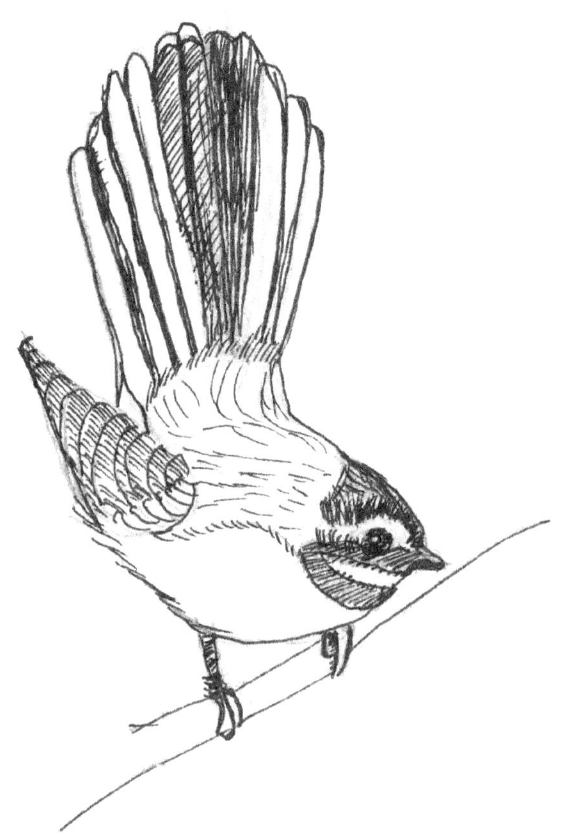

That
More
Is
Better
Each person
a heavy bet
That we will live
Without her
We Shall Not
We Shall Not
Her golden sands of Byron's beach pearls
I have not seen in the heavens,
Or Mars or the Moon landings

In a sea of blue and white
A planet of 80%
Ocean
Indian, Pacific & Atlantic
All disregarded in structure and depth
By fracking

I am her slave?
She is my burden?
Who dies without who, first?
Shall the Japanese die
In vain
While we conquer another corner
Of riches
On earth's plain?

I am finding touches too few and far between
While facebook rules my engagement diary
Do we even touch each other and our selves
In kindness,
When my digestion sickens me, to pain & fever
I know I must believe
Her.
As she calls to me "I am your Earth, hear me, feel my love, and feel me".
As she has fed us
For millennia
Should we not
Honour our mother's
Needs

My dear sister
Was a bliss birth
Am I
Just another burden on this Earth?

Mother Earth Part II

Like no other we know
How she billows
Now with soft skies
So blue
Yet, tight constricted flow
When fracking shows
Her, so delicate below
Where no tools should go.
Don't touch her there
Or you'll never know
What generations past
Before the industrial blast
What delights & bounties
Full
Are in her warm daisy days

hands in dishes
climbing into lemon
bushes
diving for seashells
in Phillip Island's shallow shores
& driving silent hybrid
cars with great big
doors.

We've degraded our
Earth
Linear systems
On a finite planet.

Mother Earth Part III

I write in the
moonlight
alone
to
my one and only
Mother

Earth
She finds us weeping
And feeds us figs
Lullabies of bird song
Treasures in shells of the deep
We need her
To rest
To be respected
When I think of my heart
Full of jewels
my being
being mined
my animals
face extinction
I am blue & green
And I will
Look and see
Humans as a curse
And almost a scurge
She's sitting
Leafy
And plush
In my suburbs
Of Melbourne
But underneath the oil
Of riches deep
Disturbs her troubled sleep

As Archie says
"there's weeping in the forest"
as our ancient trees
grew, so the natives,
knew

of dreaming and tides of PNG
when to go paddling and
when to breath deep
it's like that for the coast of Europe
is it?
I heard a rumour
That there is lots of rubbish
On the seashore of the Pacific,
Does it mean it's a bit of an eyesore?
Now that we have everything we need
In the West
Can we awaken please
It's all our Earth!
The only one
I've seen so far,
Even when we take man to mars,
And she's our mothership
Spinning in the
Dark
Light
Dark
Light

Breathing in her shallow oxygen layer,
Then it's space and wack!
We have too much fear
Of what?
Or is that just me?

Hey China, wasn't Tibet
Really leading the way,
How can love and kindness
Be so out of date?
So out of fashion?

Fuming, her lung gusts reach tornado speeds tonight
Where angels fear to tread, in my body and in my bed

Mother Earth Part IV

We've hurt her
And
Oh
Damn,
Now, look at the weather!

Filling up on the Daintree juice
Water envelops us from
Indian to Atlantic to Pacific

But why the live meat export trade?

Have the empathetic generation really arrived?

With new awareness, bhakti and devotion.

Has the tribe of earthling found
the pulse strong enough to feel?

When you touch the earth
peel an orange
touch a leaf
break apart a pearl
purse like shell
or just sleep,
sheltered
like millions do
under a red roofed box
as big as a sun

if the stars guide
the simple soul
of indigenous tribesmen
in the Central Desert
of Australia

then why cannot
the moon be made
a calendar month again?
"please, please yourselves" she says

but in her heart
I know she says
"I've had enough
now
you little upstart!"

I hear music and I'm left wondering,
If the Earth shows up heaving & out of breath
One day…
Will someone give her a shoe in?

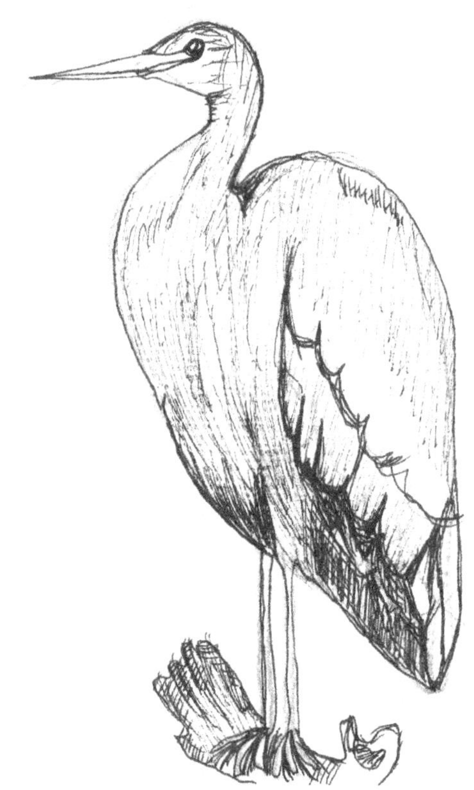

Our Feathery Friends

Does a life
have a price?

Does the sacrifice
of one life
like a chicken's
mean
anything
to
anyone
anymore?

I saw the program
and I watched the
grim horror
of a battery hen's
life and slaughter

is it honoured
at KFC?
does a kindly hen
have its existence
made meaningless
by our first world
greed and hunger?

where is the pleasure
for the hen?
to step lightly and
pick at our Earth
I think it's time
to open our eyes
to the suffering
these birds
have endured
for our
five minute noodle spice

the sacrifice
of one life
to sustain
another
there we are
humans with
our rumblings
with no “thank yous”
said to our
feathery friends

Poetree

within the bark
in the nightness of blue
I breathe
my branches stretch
outward into the
new air of day

and while in mum's Chapel Street flat
my favourite silver birch
she says
'the mind cannot know
what the heart understands'

my fever subsides
and I roll over happy

Raining

dripping
caressing
past
trees
streets
homes
cars
shining
with
wetness

crossing
over a bridge

Entangled in thoughts
of
'ifs'
and
'maybes'

doing nothing
saying nothing

Swelling
forming

Kept tight
She says

Us, Us, Us,
together

blossoming
shedding
reviving

Sickness & Fever

the soil slumbers
beneath us
I feel her
burying her shoots for Spring
to enter her
the sun
must divide
the day
the night
and moonshadow
must dust her street

the soft soil
slumbers, thick within
the deep rest of winter
I am shivering from fever
turning inside and out of my mind
only to find her
resting beneath me
as I rest too

I have terror
rolling into my body
like the infection
with waves of pain
combined
consumed with prayers
of redeeming actions

soon to be performed
more dishes
more toilet floors
less opioniated tv talk

I have a headache, sinus,
pain, eye ache, tongue swelling,
muscle stiffness, body ache, fever,
diahorrea and nausea

in it I am alone
and wholly alone
in moments
time ceases
mind loses complex thought
in a suggested moment
I go out into our
well kept garden
courtyard
and I let the Sun into my Being.
and I see a star
I close my eyes and see a star being
'it is you', says God the Sun
'you're quite big'.
nevertheless I feel good in being small

Questions of destiny melt
when I hold my Mum's hand

Spider Woman

when you don't
need
anything from anyone
you are weak

when you only need
one for something
in your life
you are strong

this, our friendly spider says
keep wisdom
fluid, full and nurturing
not static

our shy spider says
keep wisdom deep

the fires

we feel too
us humans
with the containment lines breached
I sit worried
Yea and Murrundindi alight
100,000 hectares fire front

CFA fighters, Australian spirit
of compassion and simplicity
mateships, stoic
St Andrews 22 dead
Unbelievable
I am tired and in a state of shock
am saturated with news
radio, tv, the web, papers
all too much
such devastation
such beautiful townships
like king lake, flowerdale, marysville.
I can't believe it
in it is all
we must fight
keep strong
dear fighters

the rose of the everyday

Finding her toes swishing
In the dance,
That is

A nesting butcher bird
Finds his wings
Too black

It is in my nature
To talk and think
Endlessly about
How I feel

There is a nice time
Now
To think of others

The time is
Just gently
Now

In his immense strength
The ant does not know
What he does not need to know

Scooping me up in his wing
The crow has a dazzling
Way to arrest my spirit
He seems to intone
'this way, here, not there"

you are guided by life,
by every living thing,
every moment
it is only a chore to walk
if your burdens are large
coalescing skys of smog
and destitution
hit your heart
so you cannot
breathe in
the rose of the everyday

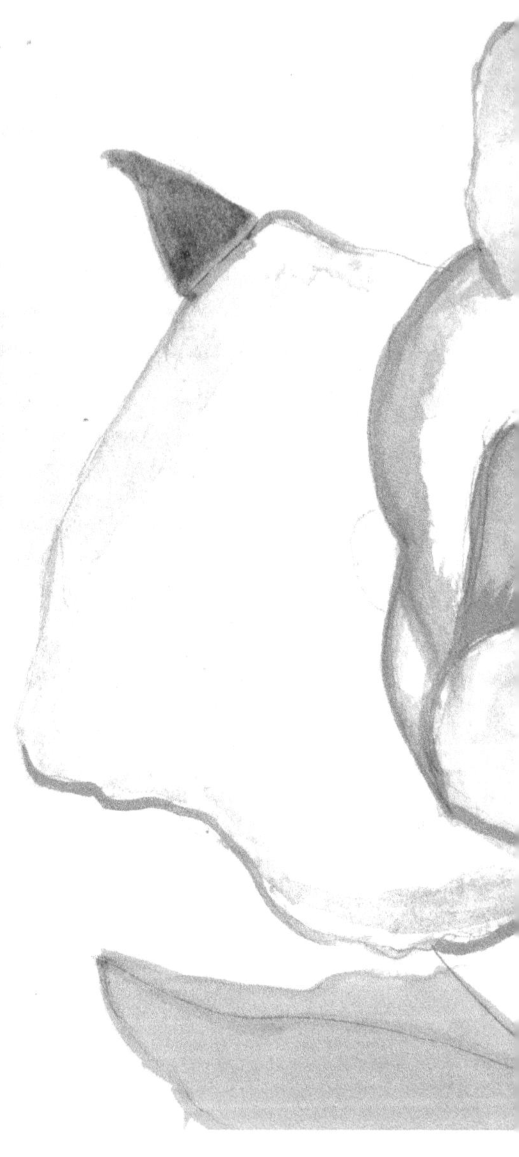

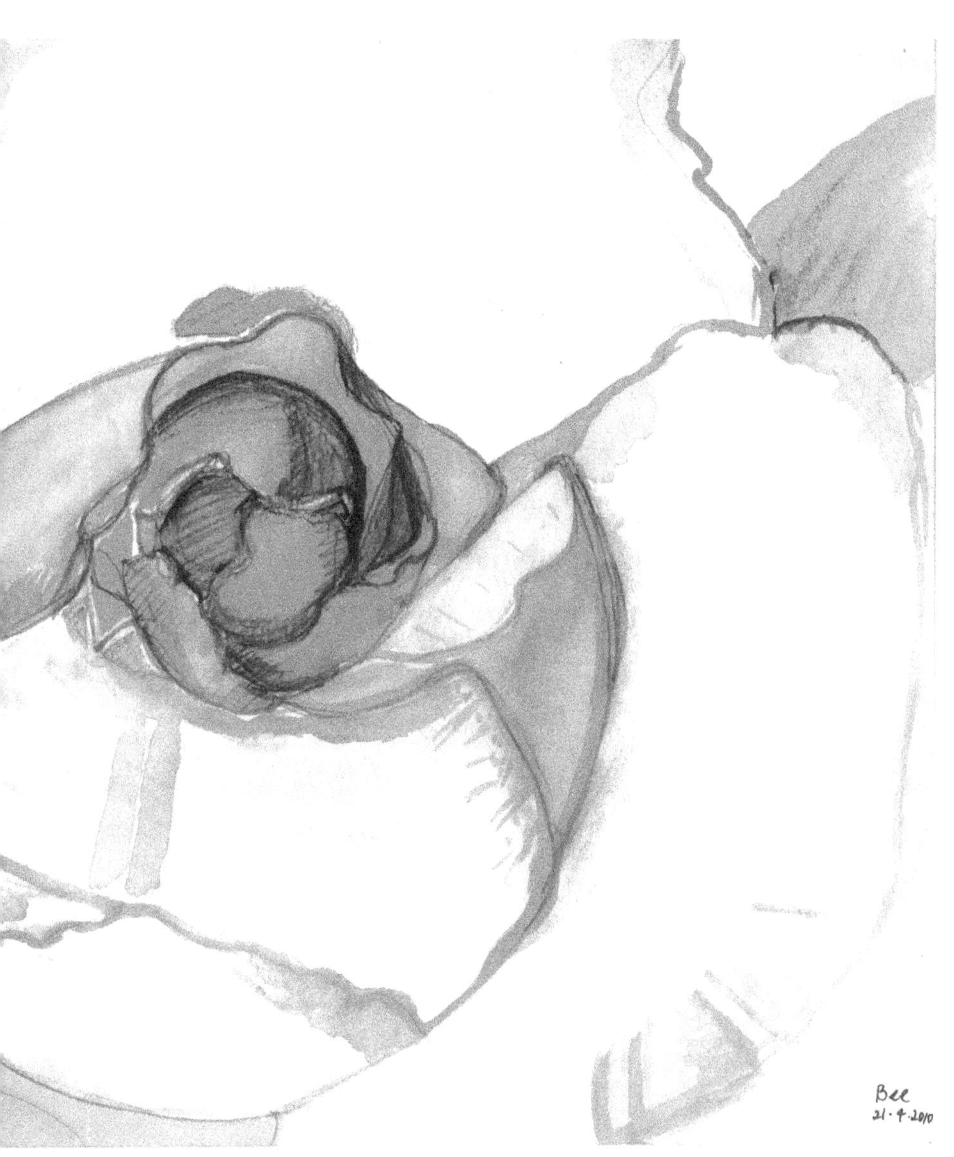
Bee
21·4·2010

The Same Land

the land
where my mother
lay down
and wept
for her feeling of
homecoming
was so overwhelming
the land – the same land
where my father
was born
and grew to boyhood & beyond

the land – the same land
where I was born
24 years later
6 weeks premature

this land – the same land
where my grandfather
built his writer's hut
with its winter storm lantern
and simple oak desk

Alone
I want to return some day

The Voiceless

what is it
the voiceless
need to say?
who can hear
the cow's cry
at slaughter?
who are the voiceless?
is my cabin home?
if nothing outside
no animal
can breathe
drink
rest
my DNA relatives
the daffodils
they need our
sun
rain
soil
whose is the noise?
surely
thunders?
for centuries
the jet engine
was never heard
how is it the night
dreaming of swans
when as thunder
booms
their black wings
jets like hornets
graceless imitation
destroys our
night and all the varying birds
visitations
the roar of the jet is the lion of
the new urban jungle
who will hear
the voiceless
heart
murmur?

Waratah

when I gaze
at a waratah
I see the
symmetry
of God

every petal
perfect
just like
the child
perfect
in every
dazzling
way

When everything speaks

Can you believe the bushfly
Speaks to help you find your way
Through the dense eucalyptus fallen forest

A few ants may warn you of a spider lurking
In your courtyard table setting

Your neighbourhood is more alive
Than you think,
Thinking may be the problem's problem

I'm nursed to write this
To tell the poem where
Everything is alive
And helping everything else
To survive

When I look into the moment
Ease begins untangling the disease
Every bird I see and every one I sense
Pushes me onward
Always onward
They are kind, they are alert
They are the bridges to the spirit world

Why does he, who does not see,
Believe birds to be stupid?

when they navigate the Earth's surface
with electromagnetic forces
with a mind that is vast in memory
yet petit in circumference

When everything speaks
You will find you are not alone
The birds will lead you home

Wisdom Tree

the child turned
to his street
and looked
he looked for the Wisdom Tree
that he knew, knew more than he.
as the car flew along his street
his hair whipped his forehead
his eyes, small in his head
were big in spirit instead

looking for the tree in his neighbourly neighbourhood
could it be the old old ghost gum with her limbs so pale
(slow to grow, like an anorexic snail.)

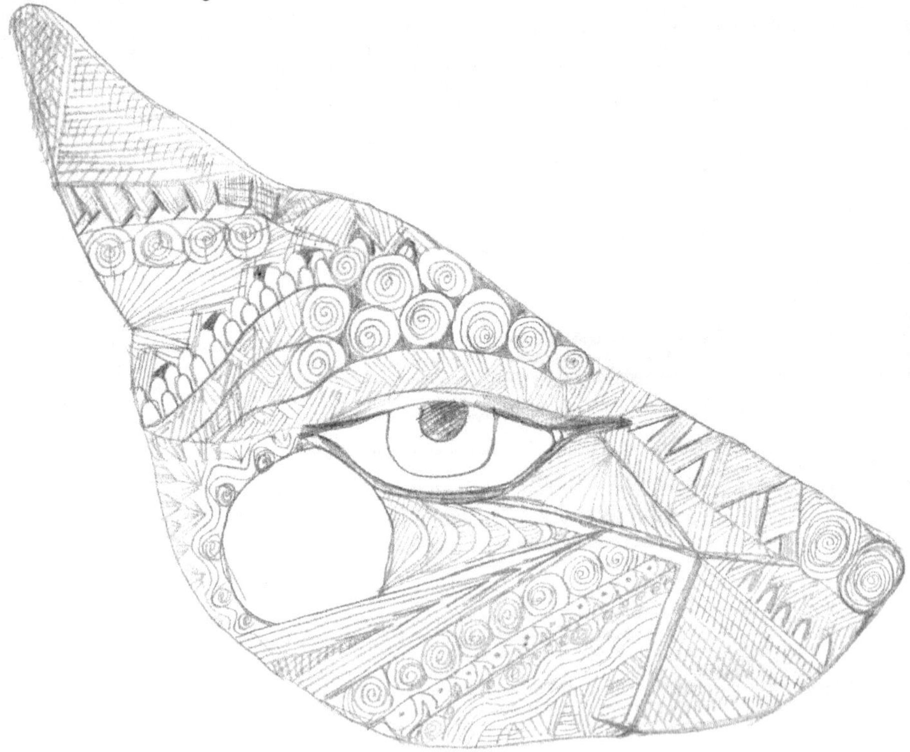

Zula's Wisdoms

when I say 'care'
I do.
But I don't care
if you don't.

Love is Reality
the only Reality

Love IS.

Care for
and you will be
cared for.

Turn yourself
to the World
and see what you find!

Loyalty begets loyalty
Love there Openly.

Instinct is stronger
than words.

Love is what counts
nothing counts
more than Love

LOVE.
NATURE.
MADNESS.
GOD.
WAR.
LIFE.

MADNESS.

And so she washed me – The Alfred

And so she washed me
With blisters as big as mangoes
Burnt my feet on the roads, running away
You cannot explain how it feels
To be locked inside the HDU

The ward is bereft of all life
Except, of course, from its inmates
Low stimulation theory means
Nothing
Nothing
Nothing
To do, or look at or talk about

Grey on grey, beds, walls, floors, cupboards,
The only alive things are the tv in the corner,
The nurses and you. oh, and food.

I thought they were poisoning me this third time in 11 years.
So, like a bulimic for the first time, I vomited all the medicine.
That's probably why I stayed for a week in HDU.

You cannot heal a soul with nothing in your hands
Except medications.
You can't enliven the living dead with tv alone
like some kind of punishment
like prison without the yard and the smokes
If I had my way there would be gardens to tend, exercise classes,
painting lessons, classes in craft
(and in the LDU there is)

But the fear this place stirs in me
Can I find words?
I know after this last episode
What it feels like to be imprisoned and waiting to be murdered.
Although a delusion to others, to be so completely and totally
Convinced means your emotional reality is this.

as small as ink drying on Darwin's page

And the religious imagination
Reels its beauty's face and claw of conceit
I've been Jesus in the garden of earth
Walking along the alma paths, while friends smiled
And we sat in the rain
I've been Lucifer in the padded cell, driven my nose deep into hard
Concrete and carpet.

My head swims with my dad's intergenerational
psychedelics overdose
But it's the third eye this time
And a shattered self
That no longer feels solace in nature
Feels the earth darkness approaching

And I find no where to turn
But into home
Where the lights are on
But only the tv bellows and shrieks
in hollow
Annoyance
Buy me, you'll feel better.

Is this a schizophrenic poem
Or a transcendent poem?
Is this a schizophrenic's life
Or a transcendent life?

Only my dog's paw at the door
Tells me this life is good,
That smiles in the heart appear
As friendships ease heavy burdens

I am sick of this punishment
Punished by an ego the size of Paris
But a self as small as ink drying on Darwin's page.

Am I a monkey?
Am I just a monkey?
What can we do to save our home?
Your home? She answers…..
When day is night, then your turn will come.
I feel like an electric light
My agitated senses are prickling my thoughts
"your thoughts?" she says.
Who is the she that wants me to write?
Only if you can?
I'm tempting, I'm trusting I'm loving
But trust me no more.

If my back aches,
Her back would heave at the burdens
we have laden her with
To breathe, she must, she must have forests as stems
To lift and hold and adore us with her food
She must be cared for
And yet, she says,
You think you can survive?

And so the poet finds her back aching
Her feet hot with flushed fear
And a warmth in her only single humanness
One has its warmth in her arms
My true mother's arms. Carol.
She is my guide.

Beautiful Soul, Tortured Mind

Some one I didn't see
Or touch, but heard,
Said tonight
'when you die, you will see what a beautiful soul &
tortured mind you have'

I suppose when all is said and done
I should have reached out
Put my shame away
And said those three words
'I need help.'

But I thought in my youth and denial
That I should do it alone.
That I should be
Grown up
Independent
About my chronic depression

This depression I had lived with for years
Insanity did come eventually
After stress, debt and illusion
I found myself in a bare room,
With a bare mattress and a cold mirror

I didn't recognise the naked
body and face in the mirror

I wish now
That I had reached out
And asked for help
Like I do now, at every turn

at every turn.

before they knew

But
alas
I am torment
and he is soul
opening
to this
is like trembling
like a leaf
a petal
falling
open to his desire
my desire
is
exactly the same

it's five am
Dubussy rests me
lightly
because in his eyes
are all the gifts
woman ever wanted
my love
you are precious

'sigh not so'
his is a soft heart
who has now
betrayed laws
that of mature
protection

I am wanting him
a profound visceral
wanting
but I am wanting
to hold him
cherish him
like Debussy's
star cluster

we have begun
to shelter
together
his dead one
to my open one.

when is love
love?
when two souls
know each other
before
they knew they knew

his eyes take me home
to before time began
like a brother/lover
who holds
me in his embrace
only while we can
as star-fated

the scorpio fire horse
and the leo wood rabbit
sizzle.
in him
is all the understanding
of tenderness
borne of grief

I don't know how
it came about
but I feel again
like Shakespeare
in his sonnet daze
my bonnet
is rattling
my thighs
were trembling
in his tongue
is the cool of spirit
in his breath
the warmth of love-ing

Broken-hearted misfit

just arrived
pommy accent
primary school
walking the playground, alone,
counting the stickers on walls,
going around and around

talked only to the librarians
later, I was called The Grim Reaper
'cos my black trench coat
and plaited hair

reading in the library

reading by myself at 12
choose your own adventure and puberty books
talked only to the librarians

reading by myself at 14
Emilie caught me unaware, said 'wow, you've blossomed'

reading by myself at 18
my friends skip school and failed, I got straights A's but
failed in friendships

reading by myself at 20
too shy to go into the cafeteria at Uni
cried in the open parkland, falling asleep under
the trees

tonight
at the opening of Roarhouse
I wasn't a misfit

consolations

it's a joke
right?
for two years
I couldn't eat in public.
swallowing
phobia
apparently

I couldn't eat out
for dinner or lunch
Once, it took me two hours to eat
two pieces of pizza
sitting at home
eating baked beans
on toast
before going out to my
father's birthday banquet.

consolations?
I lost 20 kilos

I couldn't eat salad,
curries, fish.
I couldn't drink coffee
sip wine
or
even
have
a
fucking
mintie!

cracks in my heart

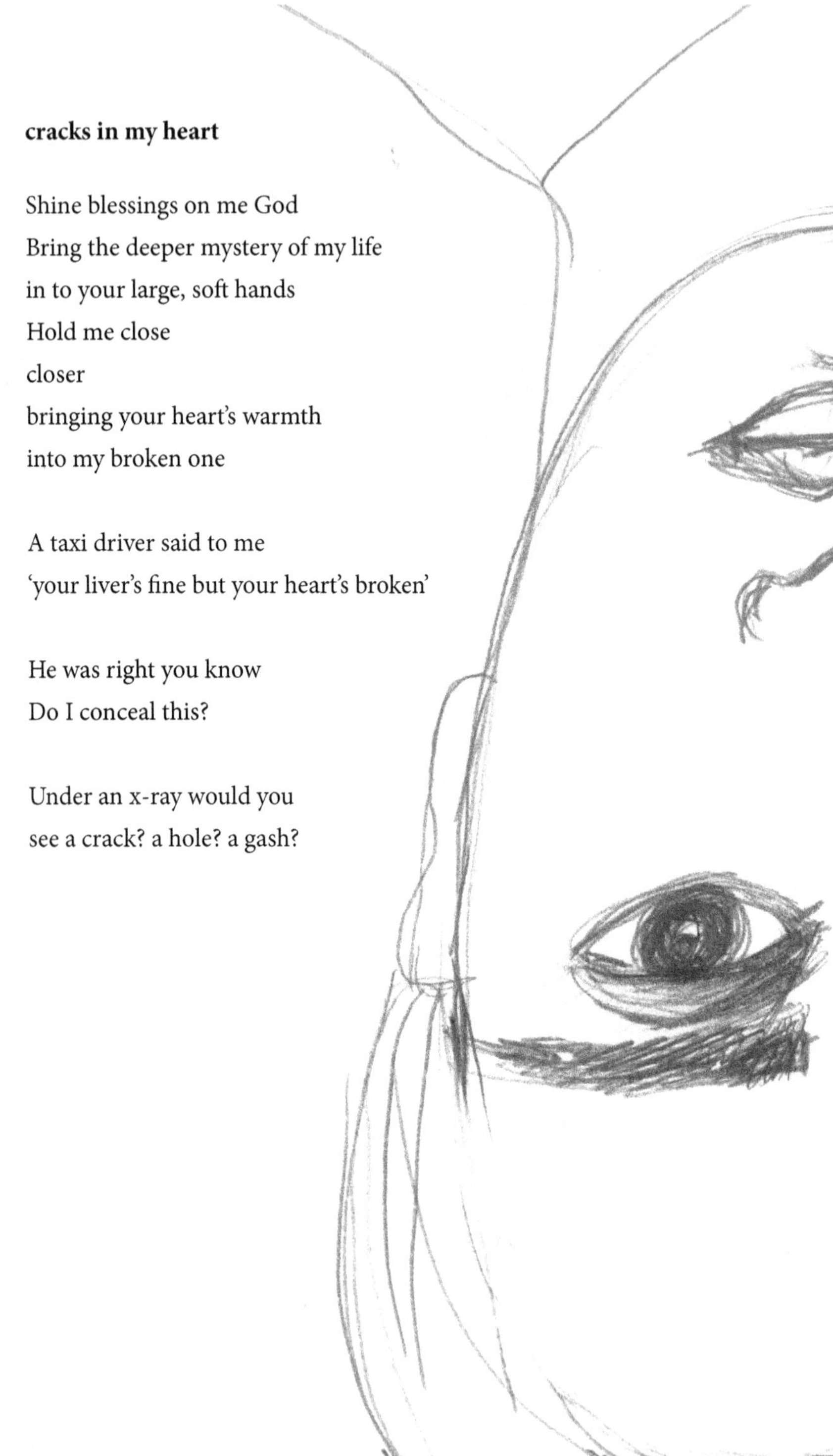

Shine blessings on me God
Bring the deeper mystery of my life
in to your large, soft hands
Hold me close
closer
bringing your heart's warmth
into my broken one

A taxi driver said to me
'your liver's fine but your heart's broken'

He was right you know
Do I conceal this?

Under an x-ray would you
see a crack? a hole? a gash?

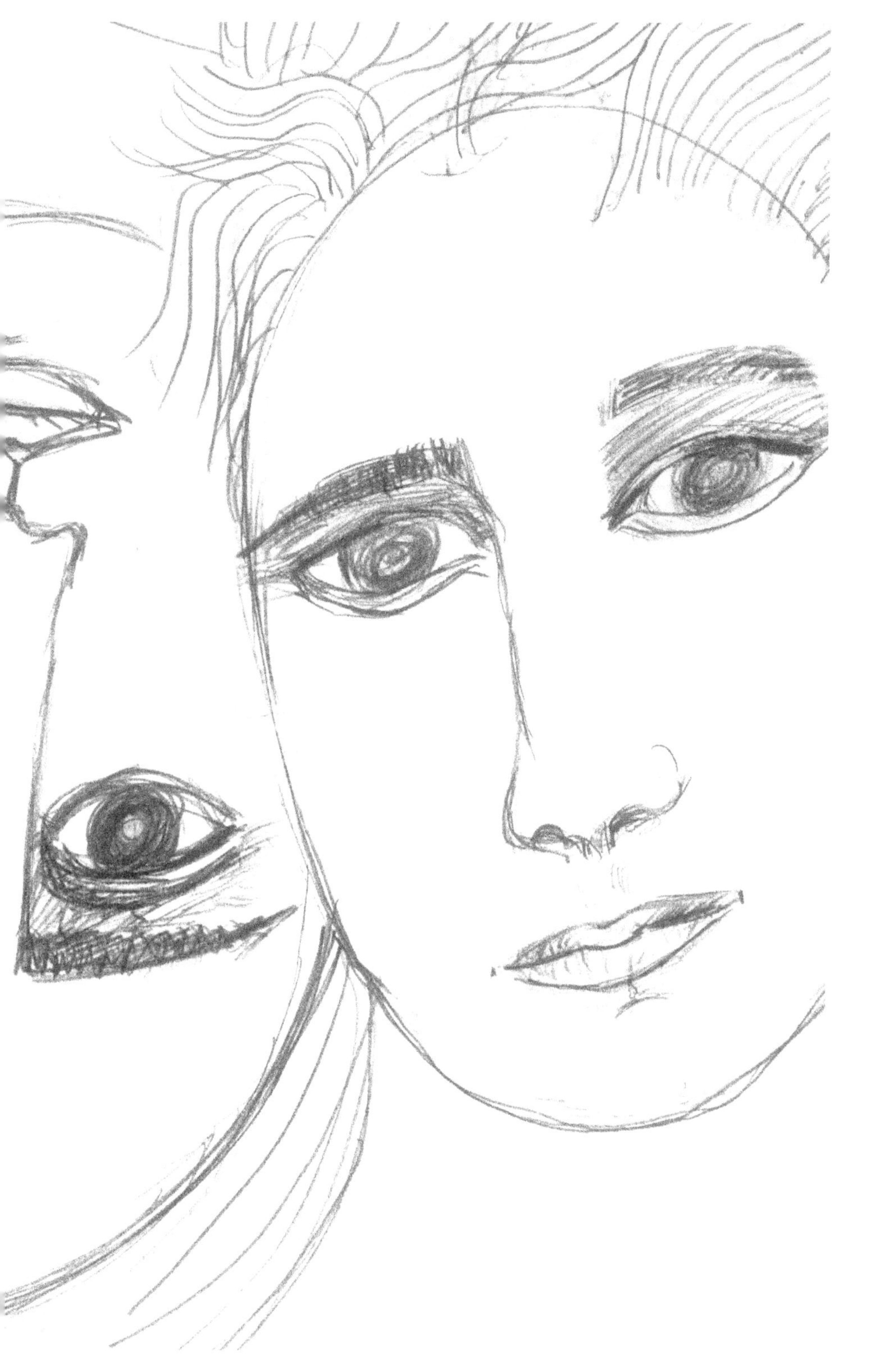

Defenceless Monkey

When you know
What can be done
To a defenceless monkey
In the name of science, in the name of medicine.

Tied up, eyes sewn shut
For three years in solitary confinement
You tend to disbelieve doctors
I tend to remember Chelmsford
and deep sleep therapy

Fear soars through my system
And I must drink tea
Otherwise I will go completely mad
In nervous exhaustion
For the monkey who had no words
'No' was no word he had

as I in solitary confinement in 2000
had no words to say to being in that
fucking god-forsaken hell hole
- that is the western approach to mending
broken hearts and minds

II
What is broken?
What needs fixing?
It was my relationship to God that needed healing
Like the all the soldiers who fought, as they cry for one
singular entity
Their Mum.
Over burning corpses, rotten flesh,
Steeped in heaps
Come cries over the poppy fields of the Neuve Chapelle
Are whaling
Sounds
Speaking the word
"Mum"
"Mother"
"Mummy".

III
So too, was the word I needed to say when they took me by brute force to the psych unit.
Against my will,
My words completely dried up
And I found myself officially, medically
'mute'

Like the monkey with its eyes sewn shut
It all got to the point
Where electro-convulsive therapy
Was the given remedy
To a broken heart
That had trodden too harshly
In her life
With words without recourse to feelings of friends

And so was banished to January's hot sun
Alone
And
In terror.

Episodes

when ‘sick’
I feel unity in humanity,
others and myself

when ‘well’
I feel divisive,
violence and distrust of others

etched on the underside

when you craft a soul
how do you do it?
or do you just let God do it?
the torment of my illness
has etched a painting full of nature, birds,
trees, flowers,
but on the underside
the unseen, unpressed side,
is darkness
formless sorrow
shadows of debt to the ones who care
for all that is left after ECT.

etched is the soulfulness of friends
the kindness of family
underneath is the narcissist
of lazy mornings
too tired to feel others' frustrations
I create

on the underbelly
is the torment of unresolvable fears and delusions
incessant criticism of every conceivable
trait, action, intention
in any conceivable place
on any given day from the last 4,380

I think I shouldn't complain
I do not have to walk 8 kilometres for a bucket of water
only having to trudge back 8 kilometres with it on my head

innumerable fears

Once
in my past
it took me 3 hours
to eat
one serving of curry
on my 30th birthday
this was when
I couldn't swallow
I still have that choking feeling

too much caffeine
not enough rest
leaves me stressed

feeling I couldn't
breathe
afraid my tongue would
swell at anytime
and I would be dead.

so many fears
innumerable fears
fears of spiders, snakes,
choking and murder
So many fears
so many
small
innumerable
fears
Did I just swallow a spider?
will it balloon into
an irreversible internal infestation?

Lunacy

Lunar-cy
I get opened again
against my will
full moon
a full on moment
a full night
and nothing can be trusted
grandfather here
pouring light
I put my hand on my crown and yell, 'No!!!!'
but it doesn't stop
I see Zula sleeping
she doesn't wag
her waggy tale

My black dog

For my years
Above ground
I have had the
Cloudy, polymorphous
Black dog reign
Pouring on my churning
Soul
Self doubt
Self loathing

She-Devil

You're always the same
So aware
And yet so far from God
I am always the same
So shy
And so full of love
I am opening to God
Only the heart can
Find its true resting place,
In the body.

In the body,
In the blood
A she-devil
People's names are like
Chemicals and tissues
Because I believe they
Hold great power.

I can't touch myself now
Even now
After all these years
When I smile, tears encircle

Only when you are happy
do you see
do I see
what joy there could be.

Swallowing Calm

Is nothing I've ever done
amounted to much in heaven?
Does nothing I've done
Hold me with any favour
In His eyes?

Apparently I have a bed of slops, shitty walls and muslin sheets
To look forward to
In my salvation

Pushing myself out
Everyday
Out of the doona of heaven
Is hard
Because I have no purpose
My mind is fixated
Death
My pains
many
My nightmares in their
thousands

My thoughts are strangers to me
OCD
chronic
Of "never say that"
Too hard to bare
the voices
Swallowing calm
In peppermint & camomile

in my circus bed
Again

Red spots
Red stripes
Burgundy blooms into red,
Into pink, with a hint of teal
meeting my match
With the man who is dead
and finding a ghost family
Henry is here, saving me
From satanic torment
The question
Is can I
Hold on?
Can I
Hold out?
Can I weather the storm
the blood curdling cries every night
grandfather throws
Crucifixes at the rising crowd
And they scream
TO MY EARS ONLY!

life an agony
Physical the pain is strong,
Sharp like knives
Deep and suffocating

Emotional storms
beat me down
With harrowing repetition
'Mercy Mercy' I cry
Down to my last heartbeat
I will be thankful
To God for giving me breath

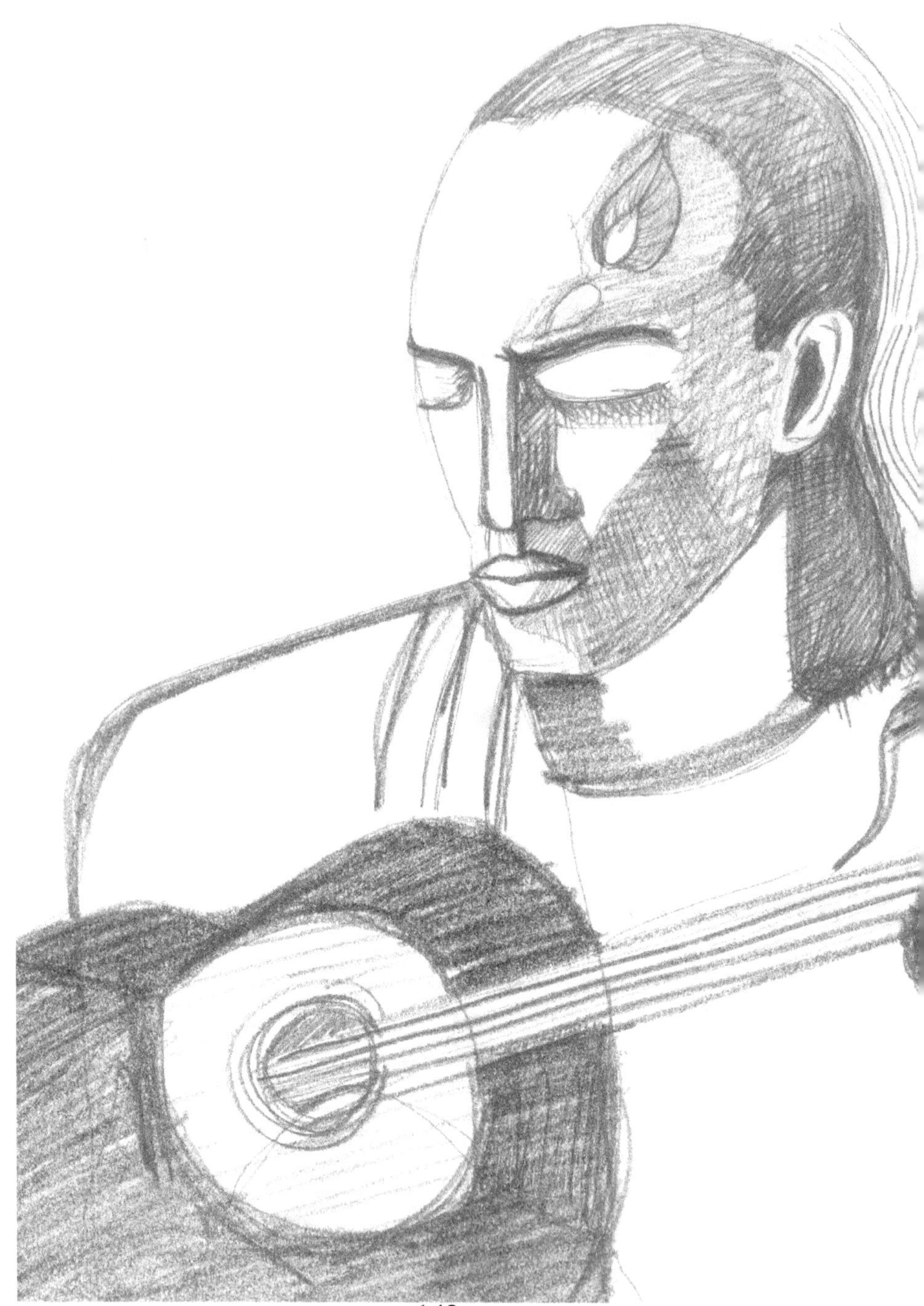

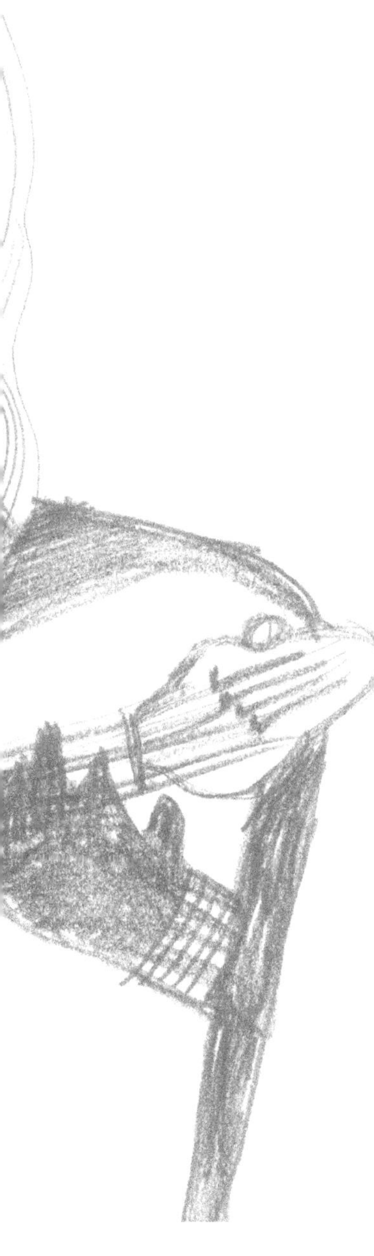

to the darling soul who never knew

she who would never know
how hard life could be
even with coffee and chocolate
to field marshal her despair

these times find no words
in a deep pool's reflection
her fifty cents thrown in deep
beside the fire bomb boyfriend
who laughed at her with his
Marlboro hands and stinking leather
jacket

she could not find the warmth
in another's arms, that would seek
to harm
like her father's
verbal darts did

it is not easy
whereever the black dog runs
runs faster than her
catches her skirt and licks her eyes that form tears
he always seems to be there before her,
he seems to wait and there in
lies
in the beauty myth
the ragged soul with mascara
the tortured mind

If I could say what it is
to find a way through despair
I would
but I do not
and neither do you

that is why so many of us
are dismal
for years at a stretch

torment & soul

I'm swimming in seas
of future doubt
am I just
the lonely painter
the troubled poet
the agonized singer

I see myself
alone
tormented
by my soul's yearning
to blend
to mature
to breathe
a single breath
that is not taken
always
always
alone

she is sitting in her studio
neck down
collapsed in solitude
one
abiding
fear

that
it
may
be
endless

I lay my head in my hands
tears streaming down
so,
this is it
this is it

I want to
not stare alone
at my computer

at my easel
at my brush, paintbox and sketch pad.

a chai tea is dribbling its mess
next to sketches of a dancing Flora
all blue and purple
the sunlight pours in

what is wrong
she asks herself

so low low lonely
I stretch towards creativity's promise
of happiness and fulfillment
and yet
it is
in
moments

how can she resist the tides of life
that say
now now now
how can a sapling resist the torrential rain
of late
it must bend
it must breathe
it must mature
till it is full grown

not a beauty anymore
the person
alone in the hot summer attic
fresh only on the bike
as it steers her to unknown territory

torment
grows
a
dusky
red
soul
rose

LOVE.
NATURE.
MADNESS.
GOD.
WAR.
LIFE.

GOD.

He being my God

when we spoke last
he said he was not happy
with who I had become

he being my God
had some value
in that I took his word

when I took no vow
but meditated for hours a day
alone
in my ashram for one

I spoke to no one to say
I had kundalini
writing stopped
as she took hold

We were walking in the park
that was now heaven
and up I stretched
my portal open to God

but as fast as I flew up
my wings faltered in words
in my mind
'I am one with God'
became
'I am God'
and in the fear of this immense divinity
my wax and feathers
hurled me back into the now
unutterably altered Bee

I will never know if that's the thought
a simple thought
that caused me to crawl around
the lounge room in a puddle of fear
smelling vile
and so to be involuntary committed

Fourteen years later the story of Lucifer's pride
echoes my deep fear that I was indeed like the Devil
who thought himself to be God
and was cast out for this pride

My Buddhist faith says I did not have
the mindfulness to deal
with my experience
I did not know the kundalini experience,
that my Dad had books on

I was cast adrift on this ashram for one,
after a Buddhist retreat
hours of unguided meditation was not what I needed

so this thought? this Lucifer thought?
Is my punishment for going too high unguided:
schizophrenia?
Is that the penance for my pride?

I feel the old God

The god of old.
He wants me to love.
To love one another, as he says.
I try and make my plans of how to reach his temple
But the earth gets in the way.
The rains get heavy and the god of light and love and sorrow
Leaves my heart
In my mind is a mountain
Sometimes, I frighten myself with Jesus feeling.
I have a Jesus moment. When I feel very alone, like I
Am the only one to walk the streets.
My black dog zula stares at me and says to me
Telepathically, 'Be careful.'
I am finding walking hard.
I float in timelessness, then my ego gets into the fray.
What are these Jesus moments exactly?
Who am I?
What of my love?
What of feeling love?
The holy love of a man, my tristram.
The timeless and endless love message
Travels down through song and words and tapes and
I dig it.
I dig Stevie at 14, at home with the devil in my stomach.
I dig it at 12 with Bob Marley at the café jammin',
They sing transcendently of love. Love the binding force
In all friendship, all romance, the thing that makes us complete.
Betwixt and between. Betwixt and between.
My face is in every Shakespeare character.
The analogies are fierce as I am blunt
Like Beatrice, I do not have a husband
And I wonder if it is just my belly?
Or is it my pride?
The pride of a rigid and uncomfortable mask.
When I watch much ado
I think my virtue, my virtue, my virtue
What happened to you?

I'm crying in my bed.
Again. Again and again.
I'm crying for a girl I once knew.
You may ask what happened to her?
I did not find my heart on earth.
I found my love in ether.
Mum says it's only natural.
But what happened the night of my virginity cascade?
It was a dark night,
There were no knights around….only scheming.
"Get her drunk", and so they did.
We watched nightmare on elm street one and two
Morgan and I got drunk and had sex in a shelter
In a park, a place planned by boys with spare condoms.
I never knew the love of steady.
Never the house of straight.
Loud and soft says the god of old.
He is handsome in my mind, and he makes me smile to myself,
But my virtue.
I ask myself was I ever innocent?
Was my friend's friend's friend innocent?
Or is it all just Greek tragedy? The rape of Lucretia,
When the god of old enters my window in the day,
He is angry, he is Yaweh. He is trembling with a new birth and the first
Woman is all to blame.
Tree of life. Trees of life. And what arc you, snake?
Aren't you sensual?
And what of my virtue?
I started too young.
'would have been a prostitute' said my therapist when she read my journal.
How does a woman fall. And is it only men who judge her as fallen?
When a woman sees a prostitute, what does she see?

Betwixt and between is a life confused. Is my body holy?
Is it a gift? What is woman, who is Eve? The first woman.
And what does she find in her trousers? Now that they ARE trousers.

I was brought up by a feminist, who never believed in romantic love,
But who believed in her sons. What am I to do? When love is not allowed?
How am I to love? How am I to trust?
'Sigh no more ladies, sigh no more, men were deceivers ever'

Into the Light

see into the light
of our Sun
I run my consciousness over the
object in my small suburban home
each object tells a story
my mind begins to wonder
"Where is God?"
Is the Sun apart? standing
apart? or is He in me?
Everything I look at
touch, sense, know,
is not separate
and as physics suggests
Divinely entwined with the Creator.

I struggle with
peculiar sensations
of talking to teabags
that hint to their
goodness or rancidness
of energy of the source of manufacturing
or not

It has seemed
all
all of it, to be alive
even the table is pulsing
with its maker
imprinted with the designer
vibrating with life
It is not DEAD!
everything has the designer in it
crafted its wood
painted its thin legs
But, all I see, here, in my house
is no longer just 'stuff'
it has, say
a ring's significance
a teddy's cuddles
a letter's grasp of your heart
the heart that made everything we see
is both infinitesimally small
as the beat of a heart cell in a petri-dish

After watching the Sun in my window
drop its gift of mindfullness
The Universe is now in my home!
God is part of me
God is in my toes.
what a relief!
Now God is in my teacup!

Jesus Said:

I

treat everyone
you meet
as your friend
then
you will have
no enemies

II

the mind that seeks
shall find
the heart that seeks
shall know
the art that searches
shall do.

III

I am to You
what God is
to Soul.

I am the Creator
of your body
your blood.

I need
hands that touch
more than just
a laptop computer

eyes that see
more than a
flat tv screen
everynight

and lips that taste
more than
food
I need the real
in You

Our Hearts

My heart feels empty
Except when I see a tree

The heart is a vessel
Deep inside our chest
We carry it with us
Always

God spoke to me of the heart
He said we carry it with
Us always.

Travelling through life
Being only a human.
But we suffer when we forget our hearts
and live with a peacock's chest!

Speak to me of love
Speak to me of the heart
Speak to me of her
And only her

the heart awakens

the heart that awakens
with the earth's heart
into consciousness

is how it felt to
awaken into the same small
world
but to feel the vastness
of this same world in you

the Sun becomes your Sun
and the sea's horizon
is inside as well
as outside

It was the plain that the Dala Lama
sat at, with days of wondering
with him in my head,
conversations were not
dead imaginings
reworked by the mind
but were trade secrets.

The Red in a Robin's Breast

Our God
is seen
in the forest
at day
at night
following
with his owl eyes
left then right
He is the red
in a robin's breast
the tear in an
antelope's eye
the wide back
of shire horses
He is the smile
in families
with newborn
babies who
smell like peaches
and drink only
from their mother's breast
it is I
who sees
with your eyes
in love
with lovers
dancing in the
shallows
of Adelaide's beaches
waking with brides
languid & drowsy
from yesterday's
champagne

Yes, our God
is the kindest of hands
touching our brow
in fever
mellowing our voices
while we brood and hope
for loved ones in cancer's grip
He is songs
in the desert
he is basmati
a meal for millions
he is twice declared dead
but resurfaces
like me after ECT
in a wheelchair
in a shower
He is
sunshine
warmth
consciousness
he is the fear
in a brown bear's eyes
during a forest fire
a snow leopard
glowing in the moonlight
on the cliffs of shale
soft yet strong
enduring
always
in us.

Who Left You Bee?

when the voice in the deep
dark of early morning
in my bedroom
so small
asks
'who REALLY left you, Bee?'
I say
'God'
Although I don't know really
but it feels like God.

Debussy is bringing me back
to my doomed guilt
I'm crying like Keats,
for my lost love.

my ill-fated love life
I took the wrong turn
I did I did
I crossed the threshold
and
never to return

SICKNESS is with me
most days
oh cursed life!
my sickness is cursing and coursing
yet
it was years
coming

profound grief
made
me
toxic

toxic avenger
in primary school
both devil and
loner

called 'the grim reaper' in
primary school
by bernedette
profoundly misunderstood
because of my
unshed tears
tensions too tight
for any gifted tight-rope walker

But, I'm not that girl
Now
Oh yes, I am fat
Oh indeed I am fat!
but love is in my eyes
and yet
I will be deceased

my mum left me because
she could not stomach
my 'wilful child' act

the dancer who
saw holy stuff
in stuff
'cos you can't
fucking tell me
I didn't see stuff at Findhorn
Edinburgh Festival and the Egyptian Book of the Dead performance.

like Krishnamurti
my third eye
burned
at 12 years.

but fear enveloped me
and crippled me
like a apple
I was eaten
yet
I do not know
nor may
never know
who did that.

LOVE.
NATURE.
MADNESS.
GOD.
WAR.
LIFE.

WAR.

Arab Uprising and Spring

in the dark days that follow us
shadow us now
may all beings have Peace

I am pleased that all places are equal on the Earth.
we have dirt
you have dirt
we have gardens
you have gardens
but why does democracy elude us?

Speak to me of daisies
put in the guns of boys who are
brainwashed and covered in blood.

It is the Arab Spring
and all I see is
death
all I want to see?
daisy chains

let's smoke a peace pipe or hookah
let's tell America that the Nespresso you drink
is coffee grown in Arabic lands.

it is time that we find a common force that is not a single bullet.

it is kindness you seek we seek they seek
it is kindness from us you will get

Don't bomb us! they say
Don't shove your face down our tv's
it is utter rubbish the junk you make your ladies
wear on their faces!

what I mean is
we cover ourselves
when in danger
don't we?
women?

but don't make it that She is better than your She.
I'm finding the land mesmerising
it speaks of home
of place
of sound
of time
of ancient time
Let's find democracy.

And the protestors said
'Let Us Have Democracy!!!'
Freedom of Speech
it is important and essentially necessary.

This land must become a continent defined by its own definition of Peace

Battered hearts

Battered old men
Bravery worn on their hearts
Like golden sheaths
Driving the devils away
The japs, the wogs and Nazis.
Bravery written on their hearts
Tender their mistresses
Wear pearls and jewels
Their own kind of small bravery
Fought on home turf
I love these men
Our ancestors

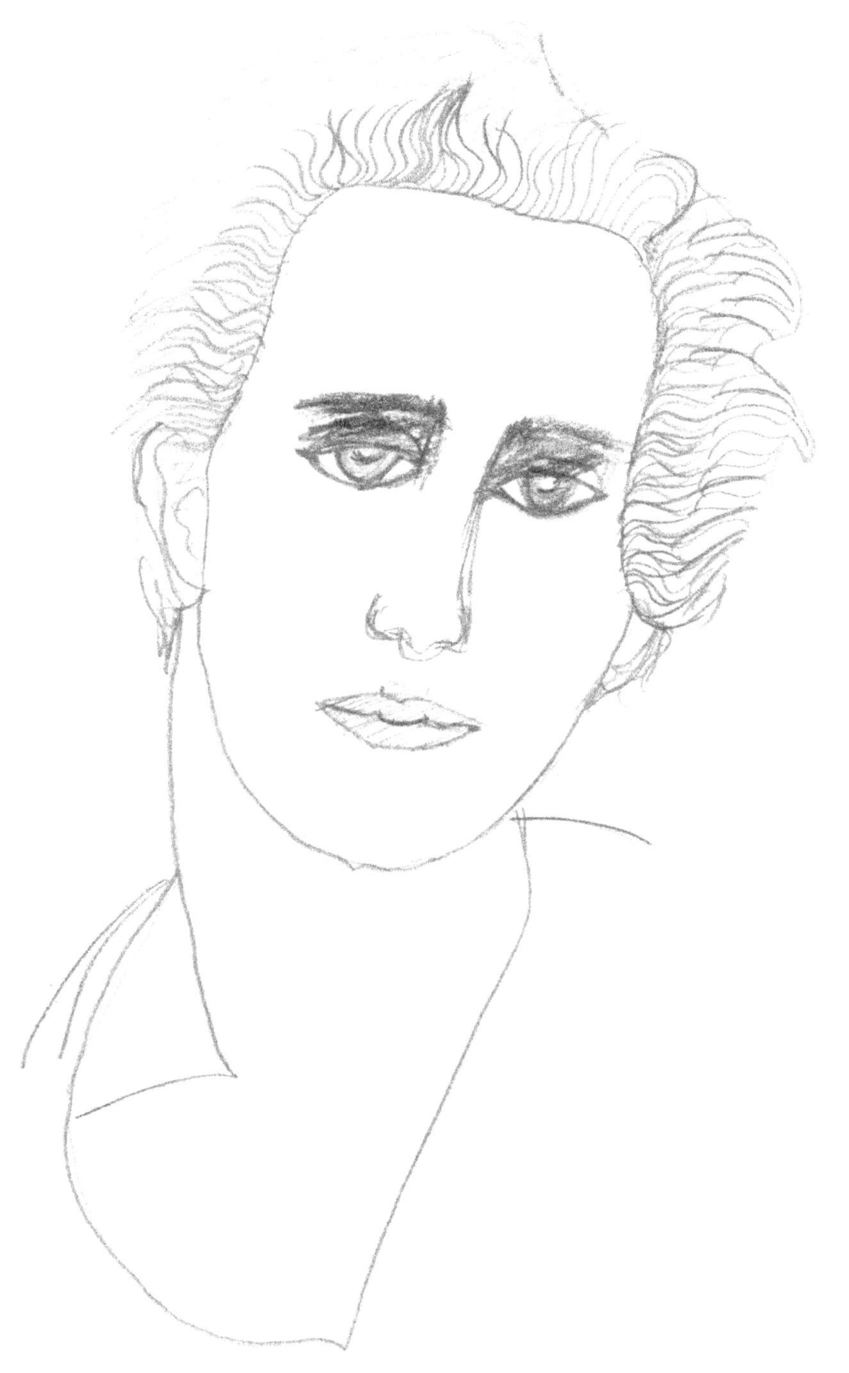

Chess

I am standing by a well
I am dipping slightly
in

I see distorted shapes
my grandfather
like the Birch tree
behind me
which bends itself
to get closer
and see itself
in the same water

I see
the soft engulfing thighs of my grandmother,
which, trembling
lay still
after the birth
of my father

They showed her
in the mirror
him crowning
so
I see his tiny head
also

I see myself
at an odd angle,
in reflections harshly contrasted
by the dark clouds of
abstractions,
and past events

It is not the child who plays in the well
the child of delight,
who swings lightly
on the rope,
letting herself down
slowly
in the bucket

I am at the edge of the well,
standing down my affronted selves,
feeling my mind leave me,
my intellect drown,
in its brown waters

A game of Chess,
by the fire late at night,
my father lets me win,
while all these years
I thought it was me

Grandad

grandad
gifted me with life

his blood
is my blood

he is driven
to create
soul
his eye
is my eye seeing
a little confused
yet softer
after breakdown
shellshock
the thousand yard stare.

his heart bled
for reasons
I cannot find (WWI)

I cannot find
the reason
to hate
another

when they died
did part of his potential
for kindness
the kindness that makes good fathers
die too?

I want to be
cherished
by the grandfather
I never knew

I want to be adored by the soul in his eyes
something I've only ever seen
once
in Alex

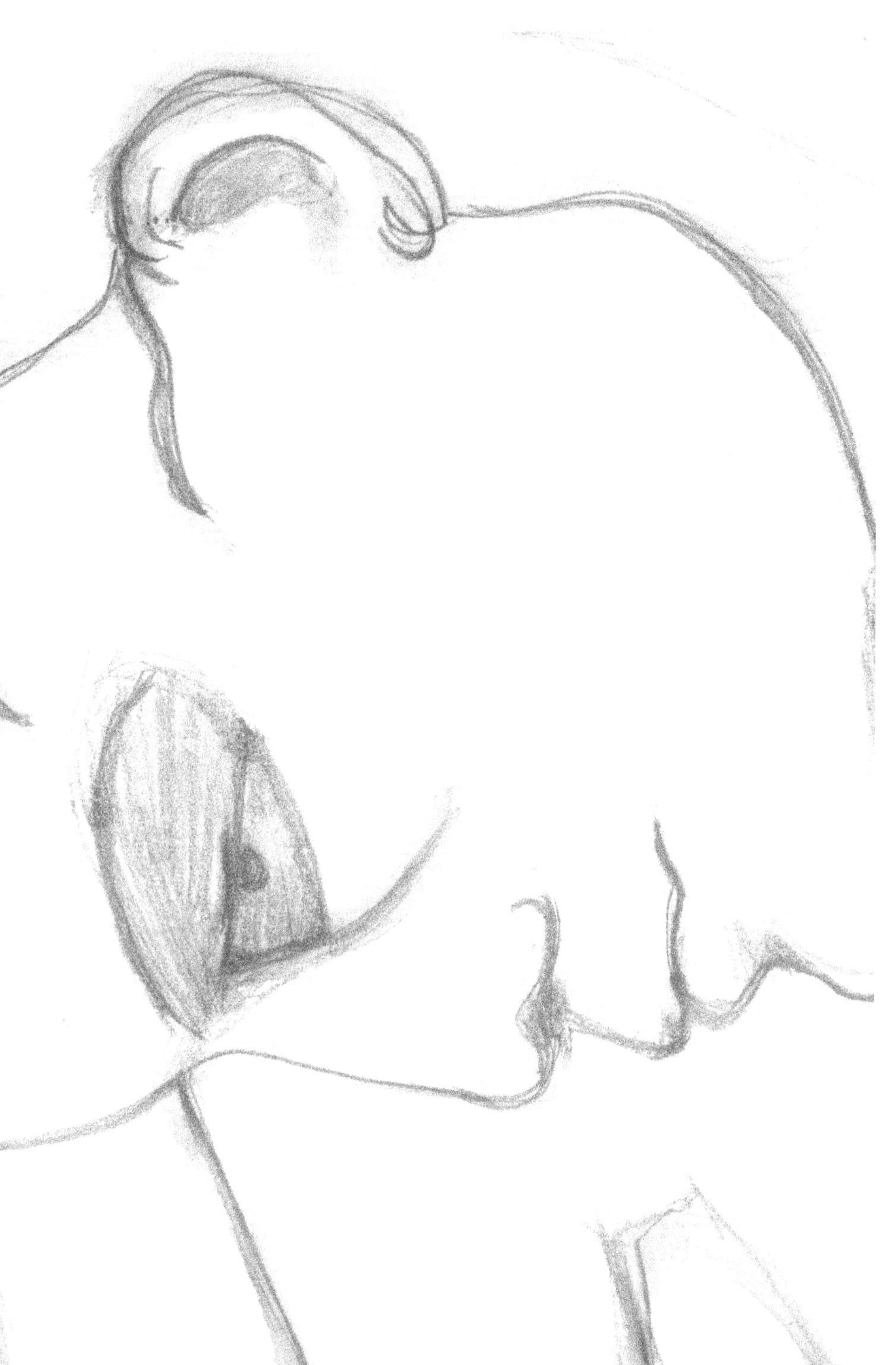

Grandmother & Grandfather

black bodies
rotting corpses
telling thousands
of tales
across
the acres of green

touched
I felt voices
thousands of
ghosts
through my doorstep
hungry
for money

filthy
grandfathers
speaking gravely of dope

of flowers
of nonsense

Gravity makes no sense

I am woman
I have guises
I have no jeans
I wear
sometimes

blue dresses
beads
flowers
fake flowers
roses

can she see me?
“she is you” they say

But how
do worlds
come apart
and grandmothers

like sage
softly
soothe?

I am your mother’s mother’s mother

I am your desert

**Henry's Words
(WWI)**

expect love
no more
son
be brave
and sense the
wonder of
bravery
Fuck You Father!
says Henry
while
he lies in a
wet trench grave

I'm home with him
as he tells me the
soul's dark spot of
death
No diginity
WWI
and they said to him
leave your brother alone
think only of yourself
breathe
alone
be brave
son
and breathe
only once
for we have
killed the human race

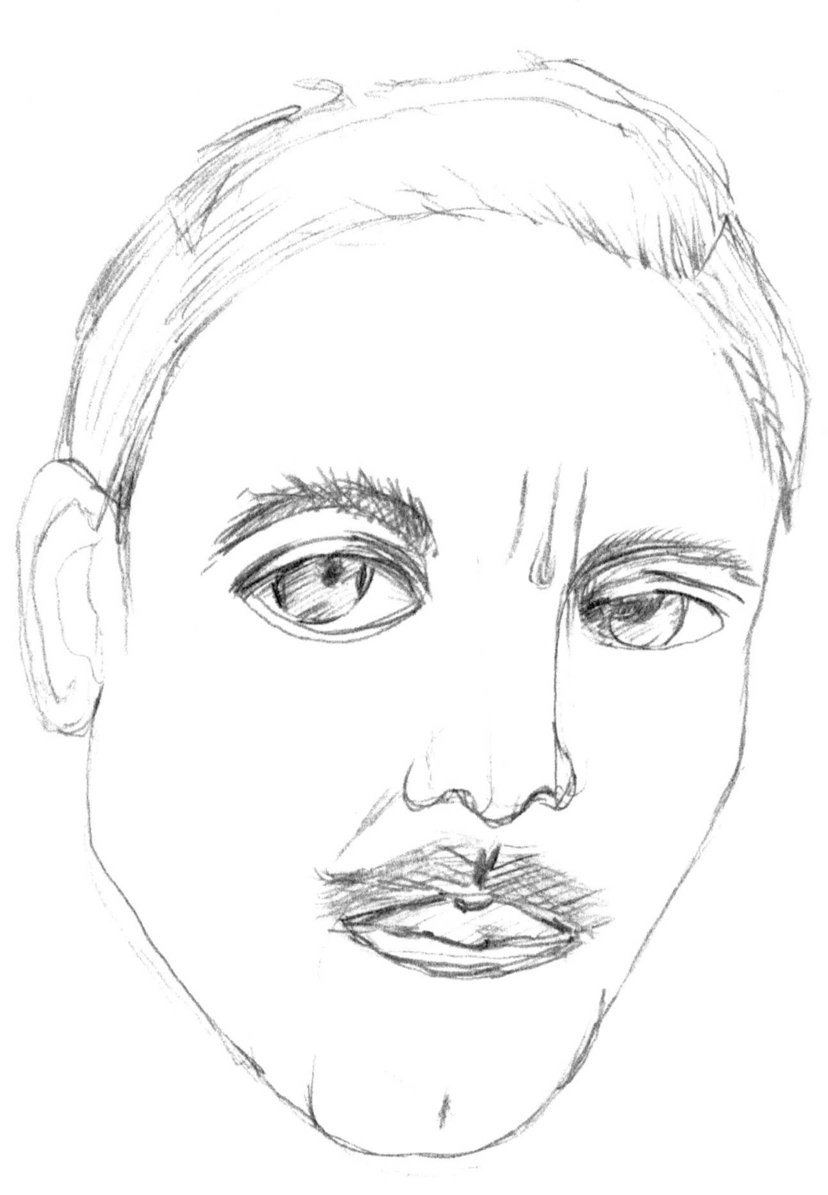

How Do We Forgive?

And how do
The generations past
Love their sons
When they were part of the genocide
Of war?

Leaving behind the sins of the fathers
How do we love now?
Is it easy to forget
Who killed who
Why the Jewish race
Was decimated
How does the German daughter
Love her father
When his father
Was the one
The One
The One

One more family torn apart
My friend Valley
Has generations dead
And how do they forgive?
When they do not see their grandchildren
How do we forgive the sins of righteous blindness to
Humanity's core
That we are all born 'in'
How do we turn our hearts anew?
Like the soil we all return to
Someday
How do we turn our souls together
Face to face
Heart to heart
And know that at our core
No differences appear

From Guinea to China
From Tanzania to Malaysia
There is only one family
Humanity
That we are warring within a circle
Push each other out
And we see the circle only gets wider
Further and further we push
But humanity's circle has no end, no beginning
And stretches into infinity
In both directions
Past and future

When we see the tides from space
The blue planet
We do not see borders
We see only geography
Only separated
by seas
not religions

I don't think about this everyday
But I know what it's like to live in fear
Then
Is it that time
We must heal all wounds?
And the enemy within and without must become friend

Fellow human
Must love
despite
His tortured heart

Loss of Soul

When men died in the trenches
Their loss of soul was so deep
Profound loss of hope
And they dreamed of women
Dreamed of women
Dreamed of women
Why?
Was there a question of how
Do I find my heart here, in the trenches?
Henry's, my grandfather's heart was in those fields of war
It is so sad that they lost their innocence
Their sacromento divine softness

It is a new day,
And I talk to my father's father's spirit
He sits next to me and becomes the being and essence of the fox.
In the glint of his eye is all the softness of purest nature
But in his time
The time of two world wars
Like Camus, they died in form and in hope
Dreams were shattered
Of Shakespeare's women
Who knew the truth of men's souls
The archetypes driven deep into bellies
With distrust, hatred and blind dignity

I am finding it hard to say
But my Dylan days are spreading and my deep distrust
Has found wings on a spirit that is both direct and vulnerable
Holy and deep

Jesus wept for women
And he wept for God. He was the man
To admire his friends
We find him in everyman these days
If we can
Because he is woman born
And woman held
Trusted and loved
Innocent and sensual.

I'm finding my Joni days are in my head
Feeling
Fumbling towards
Knowing others as well as any Shakespeare.
Here on earth methinks Dylan is assuming all men lie and cheat
I find their souls are taken
By drought
Ideas of self as separate
Mateship is fine
But stepping on earth as if she has no feelings
And killing yourself
Is only killing yourself really.

"I wasn't killing for a reason" he said.
I was killing because sergeant said so.
'To protect my women and the way of life"
Back home.
But how did these soldiers find softness after
They came home?

What have, as woman, my hands done that
Men's haven't? anything anymore!
I'm finding men different these days,
There's a new feeling of softness, tenderness
In men I'm finding these days
Tears are more ready
Than ever
To drip and solve all their problems.
Soft men
Ahhhhhhhh soft men

I find his heart there
In his land
He took shelter in nature
On his own terms
Defining sensitivity

Grief grief at finding the bones
At home in the sky
Where no god was there
Alone after the war
Would have been hell
With the thousand mile stare

I've been in a catatonic state
Mute and alone
Shellshock from grief
Maybe his grief is my grief
Maybe love's grief is all of our grief
Together?

Soldier of Love

they walk the path
of war
to retain the peace
we treasure
the soldier of Love
treasures only his
pure heart's desire
to keep his Mother warm
his lover sheltered
his son well fed
and his father safe
it is all we wish
to know
as the Twin Towers
are speared
then collapse

is she safe?
was she there?

'I Love You' says the telephonist
Level 9
'I Love You' says the international financial chief
'I Love You' the last word she heard him speak
on his message machine
'Bye My Darling' says the African American executive

I love you, is all we say
to him on that day
when the winds blow between the building
yet no one is there

I Love You
'means when you look for God,
God is in the look of your eyes'

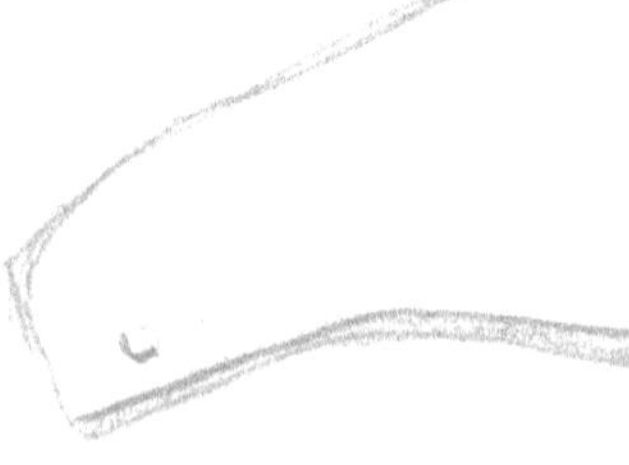

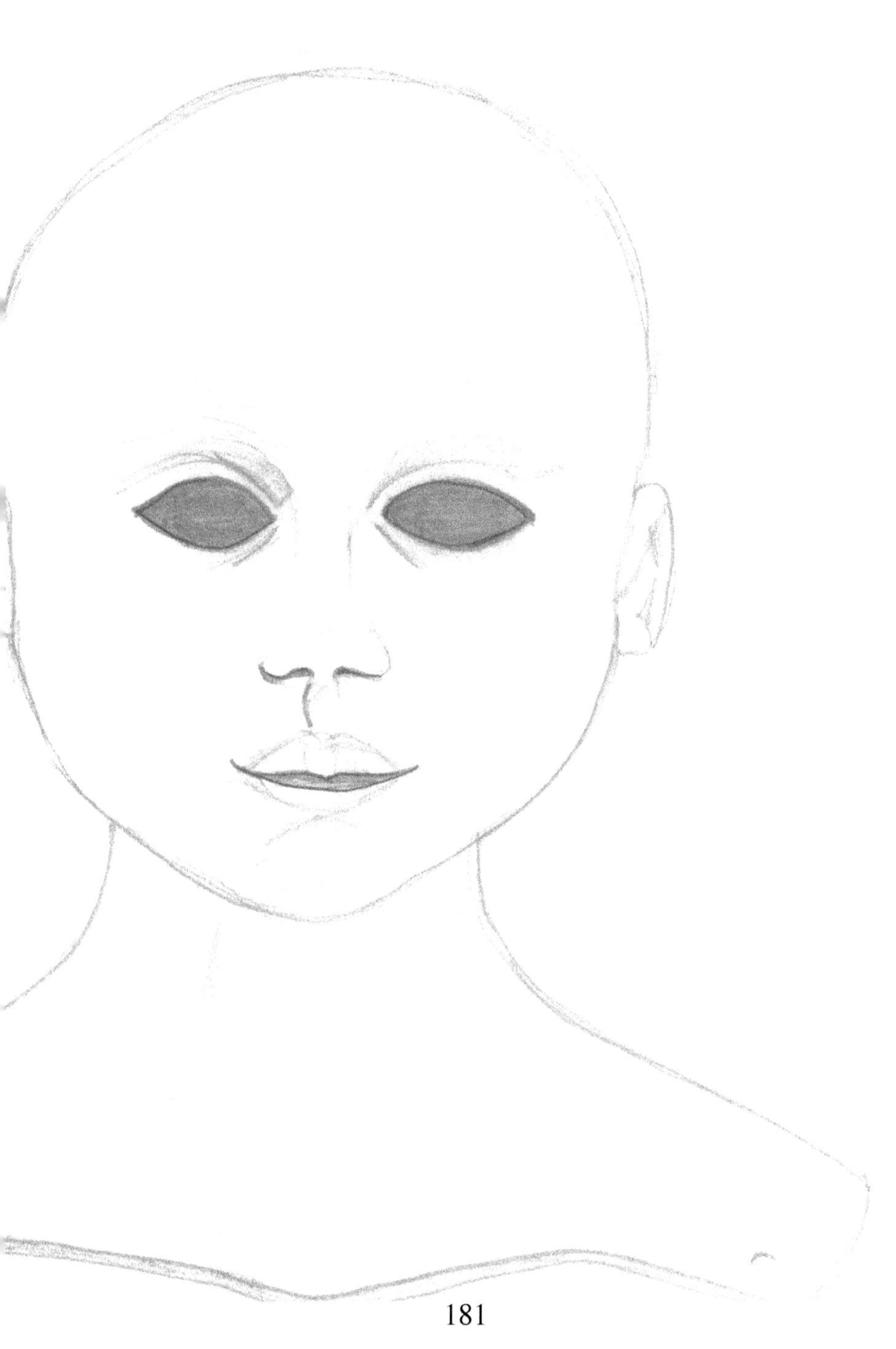

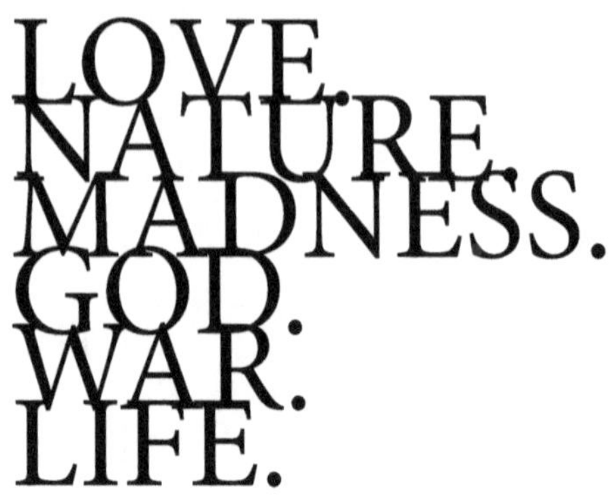
LOVE.
NATURE.
MADNESS.
GOD.
WAR.
LIFE.

LIFE.

A city wilderness

She sits, nestled
In her little world
Contemplating the power
And sublimity of music
Of art
All things stretch out
Before her
Fruit, flowers grown in her garden
They are mystical friends
The birds and trees, the bees
She enjoys it because it is home
A sanctuary, a stillness
A city wilderness.

for zula

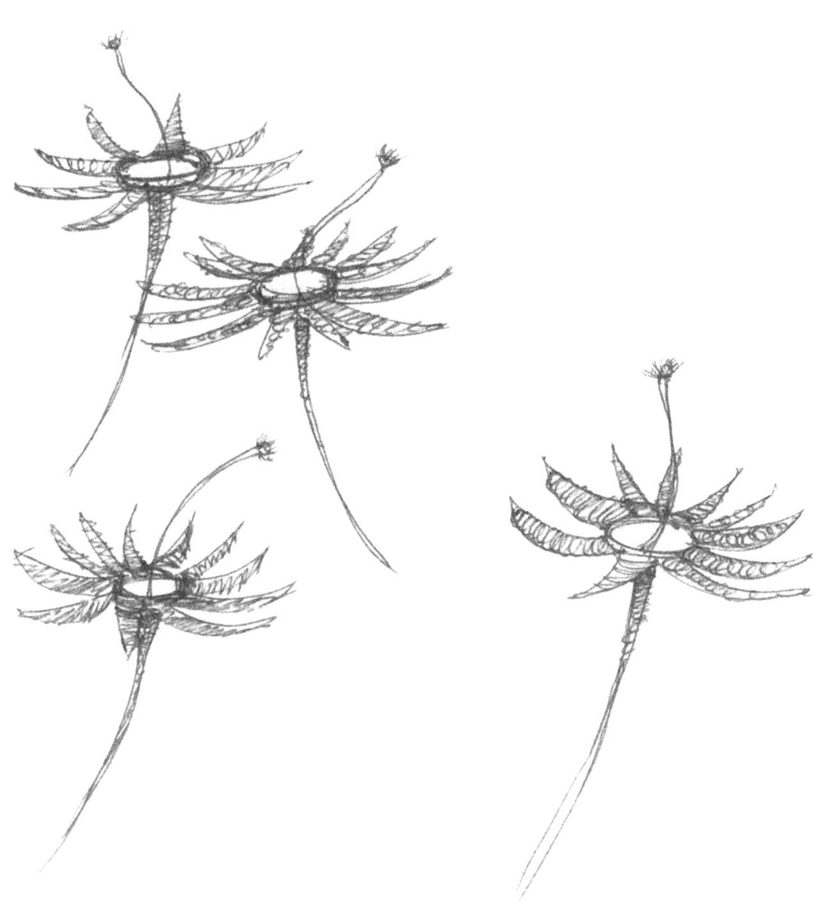

Adagio

This was a night so hot,
nakedness
was
compulsory. People had begun to fly.

I sat, alone, adrift on the currents of your music.
So hot,
I soaked,
I lay down and soaked the melody of your instrument.

Solo notes, the piano player.
Spilling over and down, like coffee on an addict's gaping desire.
Tipped over and forward, like an acrobat's body.

Your music spoke to me, softly,
It urged me to look,
over my shoulder,
as a hundred dancers float past,
draped and tasselled,
floating on the night's breeze.

Wanting to be them,
I caught a foot,
which dragged me up and under
the serene muscle of a dancer's thigh.

And it is here I sat,
in my mind's eye,
among the free form thunders
of your music's belting.

Like waves;
waves rushing an empty city,
breaking on this soul's
cavernous state.

You drip your historical juices in my ear, and I am just learning to swim.

Moments of orchestrated chaos push the dancers away from one another,
alone we disentangle the threads of the dresses.
The players hands pulse in repertoire.
Legs weaving, kicking, frowning at each other.
Hair and limbs clamber upwards on the clarinet's wail.
The peak of the symphony carries us up, up, up, over heads:
the notes exploding in mid-air,
the rest of the piece plays in silence.

A dancer's foot taps lightly on his shoulder,
caressing the wisps of hair, pulling his shirt collar up.

Lifted, like a skull
incandescent
left to rest on the abyss.

The music is a fresh breeze on this cloudless blue-sky-night.
It steps effortlessly off my soul,
as these ebullient and arresting images flow over me.

All around were women dancing,
swimming in warm currents of a twilight sky,
moving in time to the pizzicato rhythm of the violins.
Suddenly the male dancers arise,
tossing themselves over and above the women,

spinning effortlessly in unison.

If only it was the first time.
I'd make it the first time.
The first time I heard it.
The first time you wrote it.
The first moment you scrolled the title
'Piano Concerto No. 23 in A Major'
onto parchment.

Yet . . .'enough, enough!',
it comes,
the finale.

The dancers will drift down to curtsy and bow.
Every one silent for a moment,
a moment like a millennium,
as the aged flautist is heard huffing,
out of breath.

Keep me Mozart,
tucked away in your lucky jacket,
with its port stains and plastic bags for pockets.

Keep me Mozart,
cushioned from mindless shopping sprees and tv guides.

Let me ingest
freely
a poison as rich and volatile as yours.

I am a musician in idolisation of rhythm, reborn in the dancer.

Yours is the best poetry,
not spoken.
Let it rip.
Ripen on the mind.
Spreading like a virus that searches for my immune system but
finds
instead
the heart.

amber sunlight morning

Yes. There was a time
when my greatest ambition
was to do a handstand in the wet sand
or to smile without inhibitions or hesitation.
That was when I was twenty.

I had other dreams too.
silent dreams that slept quietly
on the concrete and amber light
of the city and its mornings.

I would slump down to sleep, at dawn,
My fear still rising like a
cake in my mind's oven overnight

Fear creeping across the bed
like a hand on my heavy dark blankets
heavy with dark blue wool and time

Time. My Grandmother's time
Holding the whistle she blew only on her husband
As he poured boiling water down her back

The man behind the counter
The man behind the heavy desk
the man in front of this bed
and the man who we wished was dead

I tiptoe silently away
and light myself an amber sunlight morning
Instead
Every night I walked the internal streets of insomnia
I was twenty and dreamt of being 25
When, then, the fear wouldn't rise.

And Jesus said

And Jesus
turned to his
flock and asked,
"Are we there yet?"

Awoken from a dream

A dream of high pursuits
emotionless art theory
scholarly aspirations
to study 'life through art'
evenings of old stained second hand satin peach nightdresses
days of long skirts
A-line black velvet

each spring
plum blossom
photos
and
depression

Deep unnoticed tides
of weariness
irritability
sleeping for as long as I could get away with!
which was a lot in hippy Elwood

I am still lazy by inclination

Living with Helen
terrible prejudice and accusations
of my unbearable Englishness
'oh your dad, your mum are all so bloody English!'
(she was a nightmare)

now writing here at Spuntino's
the sun shines
bright on bright
woven French chairs and Genovese coffee umbrellas

thinking of sleepy smoking ceremonies in my brother's
bed of black sheets
A black sheep (me) on black cotton doona
I was a gothic at twelve
Still innocent for a few weeks
until she said she was addicted to speed
and it was actually heroin in the end
Has three kids now
is a nurse

Beauty's Witness - for Brenda

in her are all the waking nights of motherhood
with soft hands that are not shy
of the hard slog of life
lived in the housing estates
it is her breath that leads her now
in out
in out
rules of family
broken by temptation
his hand not on her lap
only her sister's

I'm standing as the tides go backwards
and I am looking
for her beach pearls
found with the delicate
blue porcelain
of mussels
delicate stitches have sewn the beach pearls
into her chest
beating there silently
and have turned her hair
grey – silver - white

tiny shells woven into her hair
swan feathers make a pair of wings

a holiday on the island
together
words left folded in blankets
while we dip
into the inky blue
of rivers and seas
blending
like us

two become
one as beauty's witness

Because

nothing was
worth getting up for
I lay, as twilight approached
in her dazzling shades
with scarves of mauve
and royal blue
getting up
meant doing something
and as nothing
had meaning anymore
tv did not entice me
my computer did not appeal
All beyond
the rooms of my suburban house
was nothing
but
cold
normality.

My Mother's days belong
to the book
But I do not read
much
since the medication diminished my attention
I am stuck in bed of an afternoon
with plenty I might do
but no verve
It has become all about Me.
But I never really liked Me
much anyway
I'd rather spend time finding You.

Blonde

who would I become?
the blonde or the bum?
who would I be?
the journal writer
the scared deflated creator
the ugly one
the maiden fair
I've been spat on
and laughed at
by strangers
an adored
Blonde with legs
and Marilyn's hips

Blue Being Philosophy – for Naomi

It's loving kindness
with heart so pure
that we will fly
into the azure sky

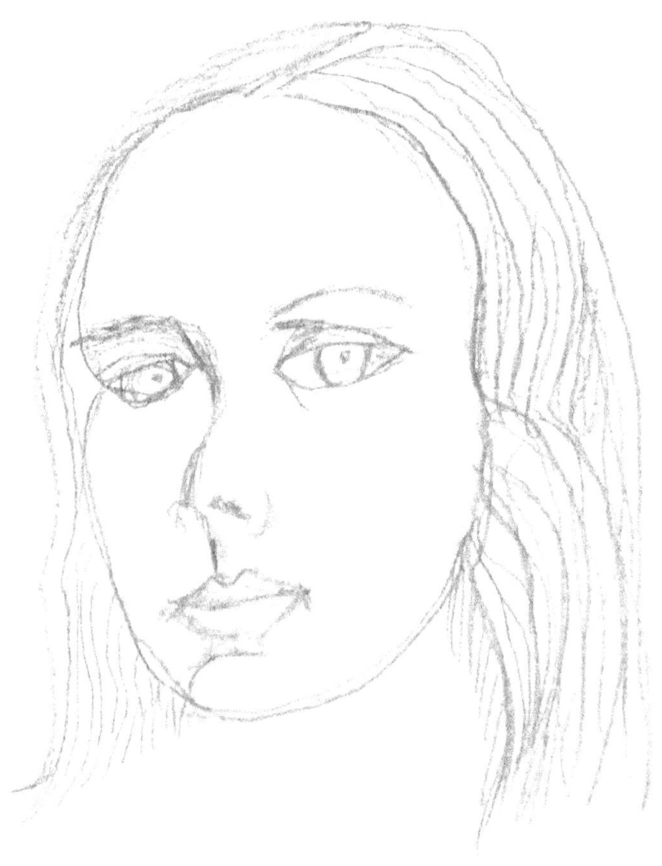

Brotherhood

I find this hard
To feel
My birth rights
"brotherly love"

or belonging to humanity
the brotherhood of man.

So much fear, distrust,
anger and hatred
Greed is so high
It could even envy itself.

How do I become one with delicious man?
This is personal
But where do I belong in the Brotherhood
of man?

Butcher Bird

the warning of the butcher bird's
yellow markings
is felt first
before it is knowledge

when some one is felt
to be angry
before you meet them
after a 4 hour flight across the ocean
you say, "I knew it"
when I saw the photo on the screen

intuiting the world
cannot be thought
just trusted
and followed

you may just try and negotiate your way round
sidle up to the problem
but your heart always wins
over minds

to trust your intuitive knowing
you find you know what will happen
when that wave of a hand
turns to a shout for help.

Butoh

and in these steps
she grows
being only led,
by her will,
her strength,
her mindfulness

steps away
makes steps in her heart clearer
remembering her parents
with clarity
and feeling

Carol - A poem of my love

You have cherished me
for these 33 years
for some
I did not see you
other times, once a year
I told you my secrets
You shared your stories
a dad who left and was
never a shoulder to cry on
a mother you adored
but was taken when you were only 18

You have cherished me for all these years
let me thank you Mum
for being so self less
fundamentally giving
patient when I awoke
every morning at 11am
and watched tv
till my day began
at 1pm

Poor Mum
I would say 'never' but I did ask her to walk
on the other side of the street
when off to meet my friends
I cringe

thanks Carol
for loving me when I was afraid
Always there to listen to my horror stories
of my 'tormentors'

Having been there throughout my whole illness
everyday you have listened
although it must have been hard
You have never given in
or lost faith in me

Death & Convalescence

Jeff
was taken
under the
raging stream
and a reed
murdered him
jeff was
murdered by Nature.

He found convalescence
after premature death
in a cottage in a pine forest
there he sat
in jumpers and rag-like blankets
resting from the world's
end of his old life
and finding a new life

then, he says,
'then, I met Bee.'
he grabbed her crown and smashed it.
convalescence ended and a mighty whiplash
of guilt ensued.
'how can I help others?' he thought?
'And so she was mine'
in form, fair
and in elegance, excellent.

Delving into her colour

I am seeing a blue
a blue of Virtue
with little rosettes
pink blossoms and shaded green leaves.
the colours of the feminine in balance
mother & artist

Diamond Girl (jazmine poem)

diamond girl
in the flesh
sees her ancestors
in the net

Growing Up a Pessimist

What does hope mean
To a child raised
By a radical environmentalist
And an arch feminist?
Both of which
Fall into loose
Musicians' clothes
On the edge of society
And proud to be
Anti middle class LSD takers

It was at the age of 33
That I heard for the first time
The phrase
"I believe in the power
of human ingenuity"

Human goodness
Was not a staple
Foundation that
I was brought up on
To believe in

Six o'clock news, four corners, current affairs,
Documentaries, alien seminars,
the essential goodness
ingenuity and integrity
was not seen or heard or discussed.

So I grew a pessimist mind
with a heart beating quietly
with Stevie Wonder's
breath

Happiness

'Happiness you can't find it, but you can feel it.'

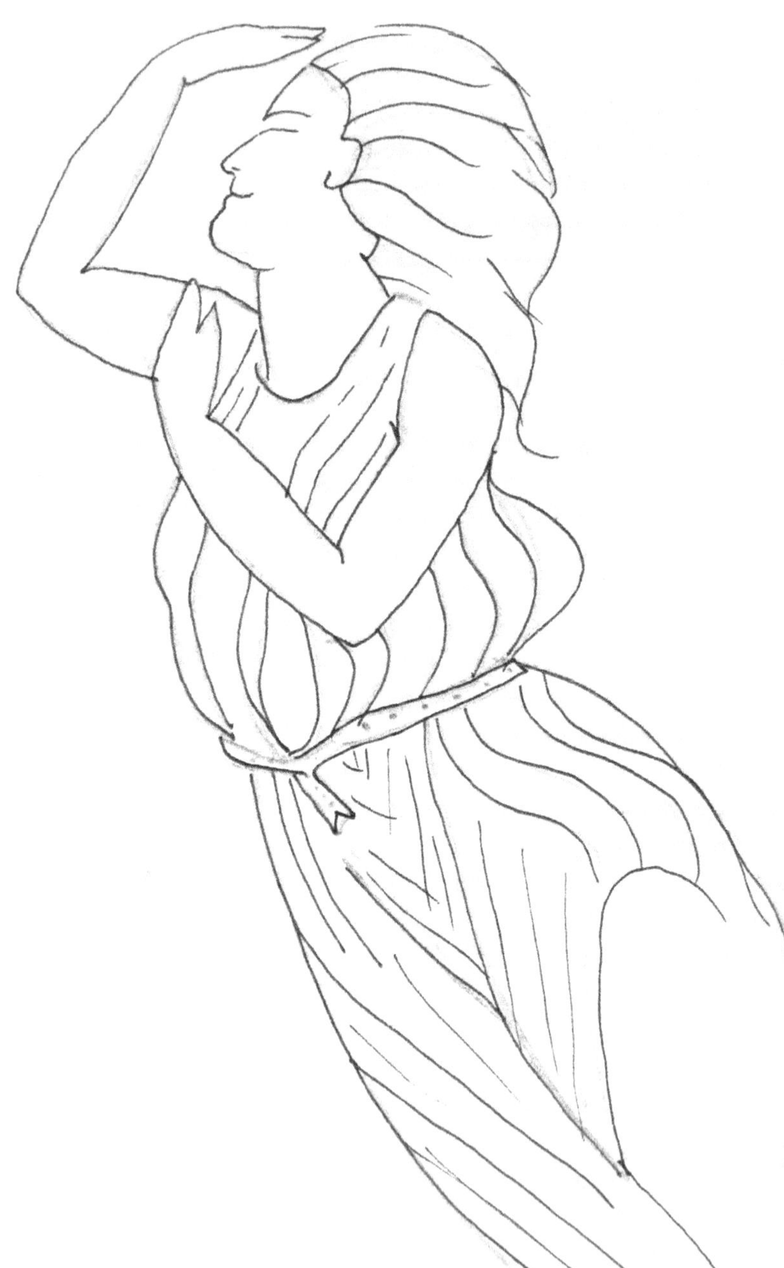

He Dances

it is his rhythm that is infectious
ahhhh his gracious neck bends backwards
to reveal feathers
Divinity
he's meeting me through the wind
through the droplets of rain
on my Melbournian tin roof
where the sun shines behind the clouds I see
if the Ocean is not seen for 10 weeks
does it not still exist?
So too, if the tribal lands are not seen for 100 years
does the Native American cease to know his
homeland?
8,000 BC - As the love is generations deep
and how many generations is that?
I did not see
I did not ask
but here, by chance is Aaron Huey
and I am overwhelmed
by the similair
suffering
of the nomadic
indigenous tribes
of Australia and America.
where treaties were late coming
insufficient or not at all.
I see the fundamental disrespect
that takes a people from their ancestral land
and says they should just "move on"

HEART SICK

I
What have we left you
What have we left
You with
A name of a place
That means no place
You've ever lived

And you've lived
Here for 40
Thousand
Years
I'm spinning my globe
In my delicate European hand
And I'm not seeing your tribes
But
They are there...

In her arms you were held
Not in pushers and prams

Silk stockings Bennelong loved
But the spear, fire and freedom
Got him in the end

When you declare
A
Black
Line
In Van Diemens
What the fuck were you thinking?!
Oh sorry, I didn't realise
Property prices were more important
Than a black woman's life

Just give her to the sealers, like Piccaninny
So she can watch her lover's
Hands be hacked off
And drown below them,
Between Flinders Mission
And the mainland

II

As they danced in Sydney
The Irish convict and the Native huntingman
First Nation's curiosity
And First Fleet sweet relief
To be off the boats
melted to joy in seeing land
Seeing the warm, clean sand
Smelling the eucalypt infused fires
Yes
They danced!
Side by side, next to the open fire

Then curiosity traversed into fear
Women who had lived alongside and shared patches of land
with other white settler households
with advice received well about food, native medicine
And traditional customs and ways
But push came
Alcohol wrestled people's hearts, given rum to make them
numb, apathetic and addicted

Given white people clothes, given flour, sugar and tea
What was the joy of living in Country?
Fishing on a river bank, eating turtle on a open fire
A scent of lemon myrtle in the damper
Sleeping under the stars, with paperbark shelters,
We didn't try to understand, essentially resistant it seems
To the Native knowledge

III

And when this immigrant status woman sees the First Nations
Of the Black Hills of Nebraska, wasted lives of violence, drugs,
gangs and extreme poverty….
The tears flow
And realize I have seen the same
And felt the shame
Of the Indigenous peoples in Australia
white man's curse
of disrespect
from its Invaders

Can't we both win?
Respect has the formidable Maori
His dance, his tongue, his custom
Ebbs and flows in the rivers, his life blood
Why can't we all win?
Some of the first nation's peoples are living in rags, destitute

To the reservations were made many, many promises
Over and over again I watch in horror
As I see a mirrored world of my homeland
That we did it in each successive generation
From Banks' beautiful flora drawing came
Ignorance, battle after battle, submission,
And a pain so hard you could almost see Saturday
Spit his own teeth out
'Broken hearted' just doesn't cut it

If I hear the 'stone age argument' one more time I'm going
Throw up all over your fucking cauliflower cheese
What is this white people's bible
That says it is God's Will?
That says slavery was God's Will,
That somehow one people need
Dysentery, small pox, alcohol and flushing toilets
And all will be fine
Na, 'just give us our land, and she'll be right mate'
'And a bit of respect thrown in and she'll be
just fine'

Horses Feel Too

containment
lines
breached
we garden among
fellow friends
it is our nature
to not strive for perfection

Us Horses
we sense you
making wedding vows
breaking through

Us Horses
falling
so small
and yet amongst you
humans
we stand
tall

in the dream

I whipped my gold leaf glasses
As I turned away from my
music idol
and discovered my tormented
other half
in a tunnel underground
the hole covered over with a
medications fridge
'Don't open that!!' they yelled
so I turned way
drew the curtains
and woke up

I was with my friends from Marine Parade.
we were getting our group photo taken
my long limbs
suggestive
as two pale branches
on a cardamom chaise longue

in her, is all the beauty of the Sun
I think as I try to find some solvent
to clean the gold off my glasses
rose coloured glasses?
these were gold leaf!

Japan in Atomic Meltdown

for a moment
I can feel the blood in my mouth
in my mouth
I can feel the blood
as the radiation envelops me
in its silent grasp
I feel like I can't swallow
And I can't breathe

tell my children
who are scattered like dead wood
around the country
North & South
I loved them
all
as only a mother could
she has a requiem
for the 15,861 dead
when water brings death
and subsides
does she know her own strength
as it courses through the land
and causes
misery upon misery
for the ancient Shinto priests
that gave her gown, crown and throne

it's 10.35
and I'm alive
but who is not?
Who will be sick
who will die
who will survive
with only radiationed eyes?
when tsunami
breathes her last breath

Jess – a thousand walking days

a thousand stars
in her eyes
a billion walking days full of steps
having been done already
'I died to love,' she said
'but my heart
was so true
it blew everyone
hilter skilter'
black & blue
'I have a heart of an angel"
'on the wings of a dove'
'my body is stained blue,
and you?'
she says
or am I God?
I'm confused as once you
knew me as Magdalena
true
with eyes so pure
the love
in her heart
is for him
but she panics

I'm touching the
ground with the
feathers of love
walking around
home
like a tiger
like her paintings
she's touching a circle
in her dreams
a thousand footsteps
of Buddha
before her
but one beside her
NOW
NOW
NOW
is the time
to dine
and love
and die for love
so true
that's all you
have to do

LOVE
ONE
ANOTHER

I'm frightened by the wind
outside my window
yet it whistles hope
hope
if only
WE HUMANS
COULD LOVE ONE ANOTHER

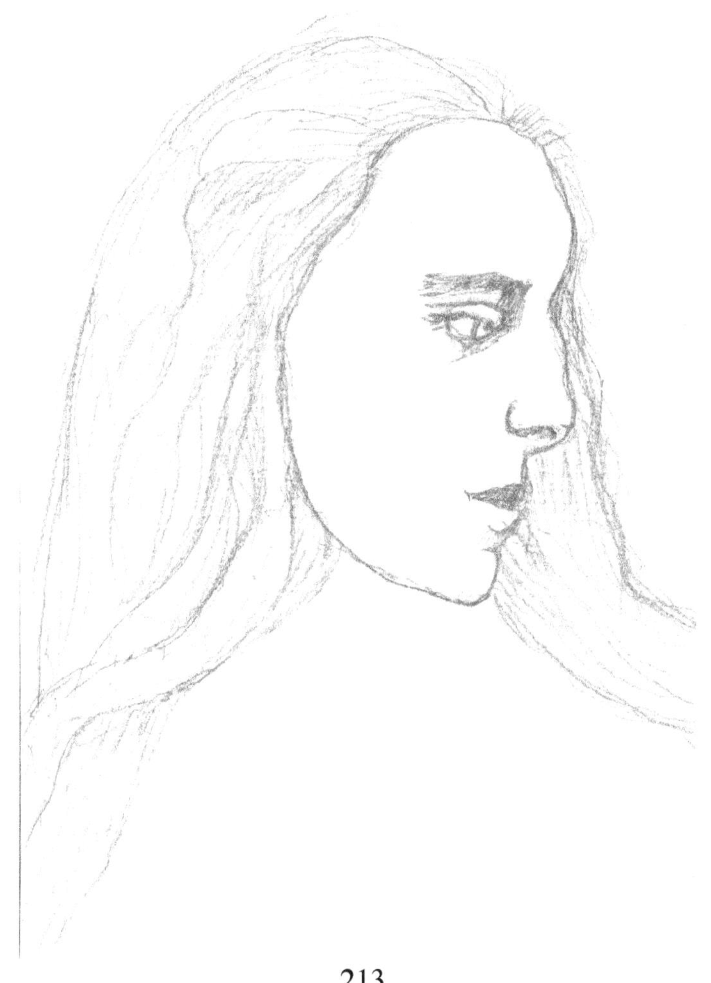

Jessie

she feels the pull of the land
always
the pull of the land
it doesn't matter
what country she visits
her land pulls her home
it never leaves
her
the tug
from gully to gulf
from ancient wondering
of ancestors past
it's in her eyes
in her strong arms
her sandy face
Jessie, my dear traveller

Jude's Garden

we sit
in Jude's garden
enjoying coffee
enjoying tea
my tears
invisible
touch my hand
and I wipe them away as dust
from the long train journey

a crimson lorikeet
in graceful purpose
nibbles his breakfast
from the nearby weeping myrtle

I am not of this time
as the man does not say
awww matttttttteeeeee
'where's my lover'

her skin is worn and soft
her eyes are turquoise
they glimmer and light
as we cross on the ferry
'look at the pelican!'
as they glide over head
their huge bills
taut in a neat spearhead

Just a bus ride

when he smiles
you walk further down the bus
there you may be safe from his blackness

white drinking fountains
and white toilets
parallel the idea of what is pure
can be seen

it is only his hair now
that has the fine curve of Afro curls
all grey and white
and
gorgeous

so the white Knight was murdered
in his cavalcade
so too the black Bishop shot down on his
tour-stop balcony

with words you can say
what by definition is
wrong
but how do you teach generations of their ignorance
how to wash from top to bottom
their false beliefs?

I know first hand the white rich peoples 'entitlement' issues
I have been spat at, sitting outside my local cafe
openly laughed at in my hot pink top
told I was on the 'wrong side of the tracks'
that I looked 'so sad' having lunch by myself with only
my dog as company
then I smile, and walk back home
to find my haven

Kelly B & Zula

a rub, a tickle and a pat
are all she
needs to relax

a touch, a warm hand
a sniff & a pat
is all she
needs to be at peace

even if she's grumpy
even if she's sore
more and more work
add the rub, the pat, the tickle
the touch all make
her terribly soft

Leonardo's Air

Do you see the smog?
Do you feel the air
I drank in Leonardo's air
his breath high up
in the mountains
today.

the rain pours down
I'm inside
thanking my lucky star
I'm not homeless
in this 6 ½ degree night.

storms lash the city
and I wonder where
it's snowing tonight?

I want to feel you from
inside
but you're not of flesh anymore
you say we were married
this morning
I remember crying and holding hands
I can't see you
(except in my sketch book)
but I can hear you

Love is curing all my ills

I am in God's hands
As I lie alone
In my bed
Please forgive every instance
Of shameful thought
Myself
I did not love
I did not love the gift
Of my woman's body

Black dog ingenue

Now?
I have a real furry black dog
her eyes are full to the brim
with soul
her depth of love
her playful spirit
is all I need on our
long daily walks

Now, I have a real
black dog

Moon, star, wind, fire

The temperature has dropped
and the fire
the post-forest
is searching for its
embers

It's cold
I'm aching and caving in
a sheet cocoon
as the window reveals
poetic lightning
I'm looking in the mirror
Moon, star, wind, fire

I dream of my grandfather

Like the roses
scraping their thorns
on the stainglass windows
of my endless
white
hallway

the puzzle of childhood
pushes against me
in the night
chattering
'You must, you must!'

always empty when you leave
always full when I see her smile
nothing in between insecurities
pale lackless face
that screams as it smiles

In the morning
we lie
both battered
from
this
winter's
gale

My fragments

knowledge is freedom
understanding is peace

'Put me in a box,
and file me under
Artist'
(I don't like labels)

Love in my heart
and Joy is in my knickers.

my own jewel

if darkness
she'll decend
she will
remain
till the end of the day
till the Saviour
comes
but until then
she shall
remain

Naomi

Her eyes
burn
bright
with soul
and suffering

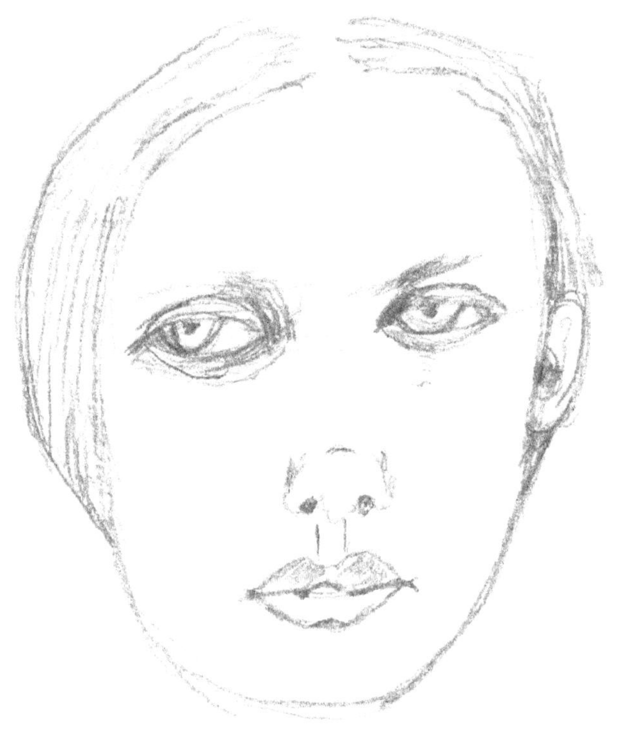

Not a flirt in the house

No raised eyebrow
A timid yet loving glance
It was love they say
When Rembrandt burnt his soul
Into mum.
He's my friend although
The man I see is not the man
She's seeing now.
She's buried in patience.
'Be nice'
'Be good'
'Be humble'
Don't say boo
If and when
You say
Who do you love?
I'm tangled in a web of deceit
My passivity born of fear
Fear too bright in my mind
The stranger at the door.
I'm finding new passages to dance through,
Only inside do I really live and be loved
By Tristram.

I can't find my feet on the floor anymore
I can't feel time pass
It could be an hour or a lifetime in a glance
I wished for your happiness Mum,
But never known how to give you IT
Choices of adults make my grievance BIG
'Mad as a metal worker'
Outside my house
Everyday for a five months
These men
Confused
Shout obscenities

One Note

the millions of notes
made by the black and white keys
everysong
ever written
static notes
make millions upon
millions of songs
the one note of joy
that slides into the sound of
sorrow
that key to our hearts
sang all over the world
harrowing
and
true

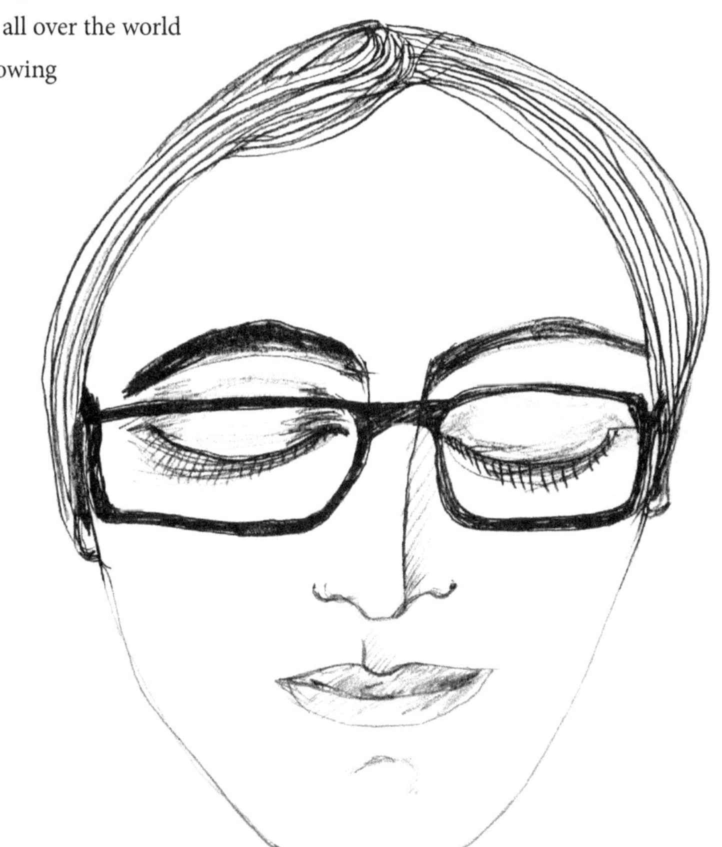

Selfie

a poet's heart &
a seer's eyes

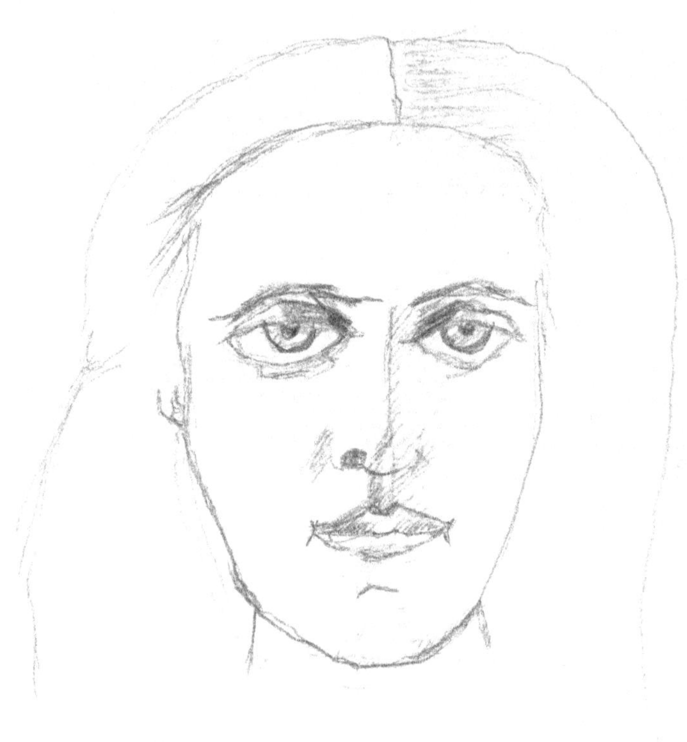

slavery

I do not understand
the ideas that underpin
gross moral conduct
or choices people make
to sell another human being
that that is even possible?

who says
get what you can
it's dog eat dog so I'm gonna be top dog
who says his skin makes his kin cheap?..

the injustice of the notion, the mere idea
of slavery is so abhorrent

The Monk

His robes?
Like the night sky, dripping with stars . . .

Not a sullen silence, his.
No! a blazing alchemy of inner tranquillity and outer compassion

A blazing heart, full of wisdom
and a breath of love so wide,
I will surely drown!

Kindness?
Not remembering the details . . .
He is remembered in robes,
Like pitch blackness,
A void, a stillness so sweet,
It melts all loneliness . . .

A kindness,
Not with words particularly,
Not with touch,
But, oh! A sweeping mind-fullness . . .

He would walk past me,
Walking like the night sky,
An emptiness so expansive,
A cape like the night sky, stars filled it, sweeping by me, like the night: sweet, silent, aware, present . . .

the op-shop-moth-ball-smell girl

Is she fat 'cos she's sad?
or is she sad 'cos she's fat?
which is it then?
I was called Sad
with sad eyes
way before I was the fat girl

as a child, I was the shorn scared girl
the glasses as thick as coke bottles girl
staring at my feet, shy steps on icy roads girl

never paralleled in fear, by my siblings.
the loner in the Devon primary school
the freak
'grim reaper' in Middle Park Primary
the nits girl
the op-shop-moth-ball-smell girl
the no-name brand poppers drinks

now I'm the schizo-affective
OCD, anxiety, fat, lonely, single for 11 years,
pensioner, 'disabled' girl.

the nerd found computer geekdome in design
the sad found friendship with my blind girlfriend
the schizo found community theatre
the anxious found alcohol
the pensioner decided
to enjoy herself
invented a job for herself
with very little training
during my college degree

world in a tear

snatching a breath
to survive
the night

in the middle of the night
I awake crying
streams of tears
flushed world weariness
pouring down my cheeks

this broken heart
friendship could fix
paranoia and illness
pouring down my facade

feeling isolated
friendships disappoint
I cry myself ragged

falling back to sleep
sodden pillows
like a child
in her bassinet

www.ingramcontent.com/pod-product-compliance
Lightning Source LLC
LaVergne TN
LVHW010612100826
845148LV00014B/2934

* 9 7 8 0 6 4 6 9 6 2 0 1 6 *